STUDY TEXT 10

CHRISTIAN INITIATION OF ADULTS
A COMMENTARY

Revised

Office of Publishing and Promotion Services
United States Catholic Conference
Washington, D.C.

In its 1983 planning document, as approved by the general membership of the National Conference of Catholic Bishops in November 1982, the Secretariat of the Bishops' Committee on the Liturgy was authorized to publish *Study Text 10: Christian Initiation of Adults: A Commentary on the Rite of Christian Initiation of Adults* as part of its Study Text Series. The text has been approved by Bishop John S. Cummins, chairman of the Liturgy Commitee, and is authorized for publication by the undersigned.

Monsignor Daniel F. Hoye
General Secretary
USCC/NCCB

October 10, 1984

Contents

**CONGREGATION
FOR DIVINE WORSHIP**

Prot. no. 15/72

Decree

The Second Vatican Council prescribed the revision of the rite of baptism of adults and decreed that the catechumenate for adults, divided into several steps, should be restored. By this means the time of the catechumenate, which is intended as a period of well-suited instruction, would be sanctified by liturgical rites to be celebrated at successive intervals of time. The Council likewise decreed that both the solemn and simple rites of adult baptism should be revised, with proper attention to the restored catechumenate.

In observance of these decrees, the Congregation for Divine Worship prepared a new rite for the Christian initiation of adults, which Pope Paul VI has approved. The Congregation now publishes it and declares the present edition to be the *editio typica,* to replace the rite of baptism of adults now in the Roman Ritual. It likewise decrees that this new rite may be used in Latin at once and in the vernacular from the day appointed by the conference of bishops, after it has prepared a translation and had it confirmed by the Apostolic See.

All things to the contrary notwithstanding.

From the office of the Congregation for Divine Worship, 6 January 1972, Epiphany.

Arturo Cardinal Tabera
Prefect

A. Bugnini
Secretary

Introduction

By decree of the Second Vatican Ecumenical Council the catechumenate for adults was restored and the rites and sacraments of initiation were reformed when the *Rite of Christian Initiation of Adults* (RCIA) was promulgated on the Solemnity of the Epiphany 1972 by the Sacred Congregation for Divine Worship. The decrees upon which this historic restoration and renewal were based are found in the Constitution on the Sacred Liturgy, *Sacrosanctum Concilium,* nos. 64–66.

The *Rite of Christian Initiation of Adults* is the only approved or official ritual for the initiation of adults, having replaced the former Rite for the Baptism of Adults (arranged in several stages). That earlier rite was essentially an arrangement of the Rite of Baptism for a Child for use with adult catechumens, most often used in "mission countries." The 1972 *Rite of Christian Initiation of Adults* is an entirely new ritual formed out of the Church's ancient tradition of more than a thousand years of experience.

In 1974 a "provisional" English translation of the new rite was approved by the American bishops for use in the dioceses of the United States. The RCIA, as it soon came to be known, caught the imagination of liturgists and catechists alike and has been the focus of attention for ongoing catechetical and liturgical renewal. On September 1, 1988 the final and definitive translation of the RCIA became mandatory in the dioceses of the United States of America.

In order to promote the continuing implementation of the RCIA in the Church in the United States, *Study Text 10: Christian Initiation of Adults* focuses on this landmark document, which many have hailed as the most important of the conciliar liturgical reforms. For these and other reasons, this Study Text concentrates on:

- the experience of the ancient catechumenate in relation to its ecclesial context;
- a systematic presentation of the periods and stages of Christian initiation;
- an emphasis on its essential ecclesial context;

• the dynamic of growth in faith.

Study Text 10 is intended for all those men and women involved in the implementation of the Rite of Christian Initiation of Adults in the local Church: sponsors, godparents, catechists, coordinators of catechumenates, ministers of religious education, deacons, priests, and bishops. It is intended especially for parish communities in the early stages of implementing the catechumenal process. It may be used for personal study, in adult discussion groups, or as a reference for those who wish to begin to study the Rite of Christian Initiation of Adults.

The plan of the volume is straightforward. Following a resume of the history of the catechumenate and its contemporary restoration, an overview of the rite with its stages and periods is presented. Subsequent chapters deal with each of these stages and periods. The final sections are concerned with ministries involved in the rite's implementation and the pastoral implications of the RCIA for the life of the Church. A series of questions for reflection and group discussion on the content of each chapter is also included, as well as suggested reading. A more extensive list of books, articles, and other resources is given at the end of the Study Text.

The Bishops' Committee on the Liturgy and its Secretariat wish to express their gratitude to Sr. Barbara O'Dea, DW, the principal author of Study Text 10, and all those who have been involved in the preparation of this work. It is the hope of the committee that this Study Text will serve as a useful instrument to enable groups in dioceses and parishes to focus their energies on the implementation of the Rite of Christian Initiation of Adults, so that once again the catechumenate may assume its rightful place in the rhythm of church life.

September 1, 1988

Reverend John A. Gurrieri
Executive Director
Secretariat
Bishops' Committee on the
Liturgy

Chapter I

Historical Perspectives on Initiation

Go, make disciples of all nations. Baptize them in the name of the Father, and of the Son, and of the Holy Spirit. Teach them to carry out everything I have commanded you.

—Mt 28:19

In recent years the Church has discovered in its ancient tradition a great treasure. The bishops assembled at the Second Vatican Ecumenical Council recognized it and by decree restored the catechumenate for the enrichment of the Western Church. The Sacred Congregation for Divine Worship fulfilled the mandate of that decree with the promulgation of the *Rite of Christian Initiation of Adults* in 1972. No longer would new members come into the Church merely through individual instruction or private convert classes. Rather, they would undertake the journey of conversion and faith in the midst of the community of the faithful (RCIA 4).

Many Catholics have already become familiar with the language and structure of the rite. To deepen understanding of the catechumenate and to promote its implementation in the parish it is helpful to trace the roots and development of this catechetical-liturgical structure in Christian tradition and explore the phenomena that have led to its renaissance.

ROOTS

The seeds out of which the catechumenate developed can be discerned in the life of the New Testament churches. The mandate to preach the Good News carried with it the need to develop ways of preparing those who came forth seeking baptism. Forms grew out of the experience and genius of the particular Christian communities.

Although there is no New Testament book devoted to a description of how new Christians were formed in the various local churches, careful reading provides a wealth of insights. Developing forms of preaching and teaching, hints of the life of communities reflected in the stories, hymn fragments

—— 5

unveiling and witnessing to their beliefs regarding baptism, are not lacking.

The Acts of the Apostles contains several examples of apostolic preaching proclaiming Jesus as Lord and calling people to conversion and faith.[1] Those who responded by changing their hearts were baptized and became one with the community of the faithful. The conversion of Cornelius and his household recounted in Acts (10:1–48) offers a model of the preaching of Peter. While the issue for the Church was whether or not Gentiles could be called to baptism in Christ, the story of Cornelius may offer clues to the preparation of persons seeking baptism in the Palestinian Church toward the end of the first century.[2]

In that account Cornelius, through messengers, approaches a leader of the Christian community. Peter, having heard the testimony of the messengers on Cornelius' behalf, goes to the centurion's house. After an initial questioning regarding Cornelius' motivation, Peter proclaims the Good News to Cornelius' entire household. Following an extraordinary outpouring of the Holy Spirit on the entire assembly, Peter orders that they be baptized.

As churches were established throughout the Mediterranean world, there is evidence that various patterns of teaching were used by apostles and teachers. Among these some contained moral exhortations calling people to put off the vices of pagan living and to put on[3] the Spirit of Christ.

Hymns drawing out the meaning of baptism were sung in Christian assemblies. Fragments of several of these hymns found their way into the apostolic letters or epistles. They reveal much about the developing understanding of the significance of Christian baptism. One such New Testament hymn has resounded in the baptismal rites of the Church from the time of its composition. It is from the First Letter of Peter.

---

[1] For examples of kerygmatic passages in the Acts of the Apostles, cf. Acts 2:14–39; 3:12–26; 10:34–43; 13:16–41.

[2] For analyses of the story of Cornelius, cf. Rev. Michel Dujarier, *A History of the Catechumenate* (New York: Sadlier, 1979), pp. 20–21; Barbara O'Dea, DW, *The Once and Future Church* (Kansas City, Mo.: Celebration Books, 1980), pp. 4–6.

[3] The terminology of "putting off" and "putting on" may be an allusion to the stripping that took place prior to baptism by immersion and the subsequent donning of clothing.

In Christ Jesus (we) are all sons (and daughters) of God
        through faith.
For (we) who were baptized into Christ have put on
        Christ.
There is neither Jew nor Greek,
There is neither slave nor free,
There is neither male nor female,
For (we) are all one in Christ. (Gal 3:28)

(He) has qualified us to share in the inheritance of the
        saints in light.
He has delivered us from the dominion of darkness and
        transferred us to the kingdom of his beloved son,
In whom we have the redemption, the forgiveness of
        sins. (Col 1:12–14)

Awake O sleeper, and arise from the dead,
And Christ shall give you light. (Eph 5:14)

(We are) built into the spiritual house,
        to be a holy priesthood,
        to offer spiritual sacrifices
        acceptable to God through Jesus Christ.

(We) are a chosen race,
        a royal priesthood,
        a holy nation,
        God's own people.
That (we) may declare the wonderful deeds
        of him who called (us) out of darkness
        into his (own) marvelous light.

Once (we) were no people
        but now (we) are God's people.
Once we had not received mercy
        but now we have received mercy. (1 Pt 2:10)[4]

---

[4] The translation and collection of these hymn fragments is taken from "Christian Initiation in the New Testament" by Reginald H. Fuller in *Made Not Born* (Notre Dame: University of Notre Dame Press, 1976), pp. 15–16.

From Palestine and from the Greek-speaking churches came images of darkness and light, of Christ's relationship to a new people of God, of redemption and forgiveness of sin, of a new priesthood of all the baptized, and of a new *gnosis* or knowledge of God. The interrelated themes of light and knowledge expressed for the earliest Christian communities ultimate reality of baptism. The Letter to the Hebrews describes baptism as an *illumination* or *enlightenment* which is a permanent and "once-for-all" occurrence (see Heb 6:3–4; 10:32). Through the forgiveness of sin which comes from the waters of baptism light is given and the Spirit is poured out. Justin Martyr later was to echo this essential understanding of baptism by naming it "illumination" *(photismos).*

After the New Testament period the thread of catechetical and ritual continuity can be traced in the various manuals of church order that began to appear in the second and third centuries. The earliest of these, the *Didache,*[5] demonstrates that definite forms of instruction had already developed before the end of the first century. The moral teaching of the "Two Ways" presented in the *Didache* is substantially Jewish teaching interspersed with glosses of Christian origin, notably from Matthew's account of the Sermon on the Mount. With regard to baptism, we learn that it is only to be given after "public instruction on all these points" (i.e., the way of life and the way of death contained in chapters 1–5). The *Didache* specifies that candidates are to be baptized in running water "in the name of the Father and of the Son and of the Holy Spirit" (7:1). Prebaptismal fasts are prescribed for candidates, ministers, and "any others who can" (7:4). The writings of the *didachist* witness to the importance of moral conversion as an expression of adherence to Christ.

DEVELOPMENT
OF THE
TECHUMENATE

Justin Martyr, a Syrian lay Christian philosopher and teacher, describes the initiation of new members into the Church at Rome about A.D. 150. In the *First Apology,* one of his many writings in which he defends and explains the truth of Christianity, he attempted to speak to his contemporaries

---

[5] "The Teaching of the Twelve Apostles," commonly called the *Didache,* is a second century church manual containing a code of Christian morals and a manual of church order. It comes out of the Church in Alexandria.

in the philosophical and religious language of the age in which he lived.

> How we dedicated ourselves to God when we were made new through Christ I will explain. . . . Those who are persuaded and believe the things we teach and say are true, and promise that they can live accordingly are instructed to pray and beseech God with fasting for the remission of past sins, while we pray and fast along with them. Then they are brought by us where there is water and are reborn by the same manner of birth by which we ourselves were reborn, for they are then washed in the water with the name of God the Father and Master of all, and of our Savior Jesus Christ, and of the Holy Spirit.[6]

In this account preparation for incorporation into Christ was clearly the responsibility of both the candidate and the local Church. On the candidates' part a twofold response was required: faith and the promise to live according to the gospel way. On the part of the Church, baptism was preceded by a period of community fasting for the forgiveness of the candidates' sins.

Toward the beginning of the third century, Tertullian, a lay catechist in Carthage, refers to those preparing for baptism as catechumini. *The Treatise on the Apostolic Tradition*[7] by St. Hippolytus of Rome, dating from this same period, offers a description of a developed ecclesial catechumenate.

Notable in the process were the criteria for admission. After initial evangelization, candidates were examined less on their understanding of the faith than on its impact on their lives. They were questioned on their state of life and manner of living (16:2) and on their crafts and professions (16:3). Those whose life styles or professions were contrary to gospel values (artists who made idols, gladiators or those who taught them how to fight, prostitutes, etc.) had to turn from these pursuits

---

[6] "The First Apology of Justin, the Martyr," no. 61 from the collection *Early Christian Fathers* edited by Cyril C. Richardson, et al. (New York: Macmillan Publishing Co., 1970), p. 282. On Justin's teaching about baptism as illumination, see John A. Gurrieri, "The New Language of Christian Initiation," in *Liturgy* 4:1 (Winter 1983): 16–17.

[7] "The Treatise on the Apostolic Tradition of St. Hippolytus of Rome" is a third century manual of church order written to guard "the tradition which has remained until now." A critical edition of this text was published by Dom Gregory Dix, OSB (London: S.P.C.K., 1968).

or be rejected. The witness of Christian sponsors to this conversion was required.

Once enrolled in the catechumenate, candidates became "hearers" of the Word. The lengthy catechumenate lasted approximately three years in most cases. Regular sessions were held for the catechumens and included instructions, prayer, a laying on of hands by the catechist, and a dismissal.

Instruction during this period dealt with the principles of Christian life presented from the Scriptures. In addition, catechumens were present at the Liturgy of the Word with the faithful. Origen, director of a catechetical school in Alexandria, organized this initial instruction from the books of Esther, Judith, Tobias, and the Wisdom literature of the Old Testament.[8] Athanasius added early Christian writings, notably the *Didache* and the *Shepherd of Hermas,* to this list for catechumens in Alexandria. Of interest, prayer over the catechumens with the laying on of hands was to be done whether the catechist was a cleric or a lay person.

As this stage of the catechumenate drew to a close, candidates were once again examined on their way of life. After those who presented them offered testimony on the candidates' behalf, their names were enrolled. In the East those admitted to this second stage were called "those who were to be given the light," the *photizomenoi*; in the West they were referred to as the *competentes* or the elect. Their preparation consisted of daily instruction on salvation history and on the Apostles' Creed, accompanied by a laying on of hands and an exorcism.

Finally, on the Thursday before Easter they were instructed to bathe. This was followed by a fast on Friday and Saturday. The following day candidates gathered with the bishop, the ordinary minister of the sacraments of initiation, who laid hands on them and prayed together with them. After spending the whole night in vigil, the prebaptismal rites of renunciation of Satan and anointing with the oil of exorcism were celebrated. Water baptism consisted of a triple immersion following a triple profession of faith in Father, Son, and Spirit. Baptism was followed by a second anointing after which the

---

[8] Joseph Jungmann, "Catechumenate," *New Catholic Encyclopedia*, vol. III, p. 238.

candidate was clothed and led into the midst of the assembly. There the bishop laid hands on each candidate and anointed him/her with the oil of thanksgiving. The newly baptized then joined the community in prayer, in the peace, and in the Eucharist for the first time. The liturgy described by Hippolytus contains the substance of the rite used by the Fathers of the Church a century later.

The third century heritage includes another significant text that would influence the Fathers of the Church, Tertullian's *De Baptismo*.[9] While not itself a catechetical document, this treatise is a reflection of the evangelical tradition of the past and the prototype of the mystagogical catecheses[10] that would follow. In his treatise Tertullian, having defended baptismal praxis against a contemporary heresy, develops four points: (1) a commentary on the baptismal rites, (2) the typology of the sacrament in the Old and New Testaments, (3) a response to theological difficulties, and (4) directions on baptismal discipline.

Several Fathers of the Church in subsequent centuries follow Tertullian's method.

The Edict of Milan (313) ushered in a new era for Christians. With the mass conversions that followed, the catechumenal structure of the previous centuries could no longer meet the situation. Since Christianity had become the religion of the empire, many pagans desired to become Christians for social or political reasons that had little to do with an experience of conversion and faith. At times, persons were received as catechumens without adequate instruction or preparation. Because upon becoming a catechumen one became a Christian, some remained catechumens for many years. Added to this, the stern penitential discipline for those who had committed serious sin after baptism contributed to the postponement of baptism. Even in Christian families where children were enrolled in the catechumenate at an early age, baptism was sometimes postponed to adulthood. This category included

---

[9] Cf. Alexander Roberts, D.D., and James Donalson, LL.D., "On Baptism," *The Writing of Tertullian*, Ante-Nicean Christian Library, vol. 11, pp. 234–244.

[10] The mystagogical catecheses of the patristic era were the postbaptismal instructions imparted to the neophytes to explain the meaning of the mysteries celebrated in the liturgy of their initiation.

such noteworthy Christians as Augustine and John Chrysostom.

These conditions led to a serious decline within the catechumenate. Catechumens continued to participate in the Liturgy of the Word on Sunday; however, the catechumenate proper in which candidates gathered regularly for instruction and prayer gradually disappeared. Moreover, the duration of the catechumenate was indefinite. It lasted anywhere from two years to a lifetime. True faith and conversion required for admission to the catechumenate were not always verified prior to admission.[11] Some presbyters admitted those who professed to have faith but did not evidence it in a Christian way of life.

The process of Christian initiation was adapted to meet the new situation. The Fathers of the Church strove to correct the abuses of the era by insisting on adequate preliminary instruction prior to reception of catechumens. St. Augustine's *De Catechizandis Rudibus* is an example of the efforts of the Church in the West to see to the solid instruction of pagans who sought admission to the Church. It outlines for the catechists principles of catechesis and offers model lessons. The catechist's task was to lead the candidates to both the understanding of the doctrines of the faith and to its expression in faith, hope, and love. When the motives of the candidates were judged to be true, the catechist instructed them using the story of salvation from creation and the fall through the Christ event to the final judgment. In the East, Gregory of Nyssa outlines a similar catechetical plan in his *Oratio catechetica*.

Having completed their preliminary instruction and accepted the faith, candidates were received as catechumens. Rich liturgical development characterized the patristic era. The rite of reception of catechumens included the *sacramentum salis* and a signing of the forehead, thus claiming the candidates for Christ.[12] Salt was given to the catechumens, often in the form of salted bread, prefiguring the sacred eucharistic meal. The presider then breathed upon the candidates.

---

[11] Dujarier, *A History of the Catechumenate*, pp. 85–89.
[12] Jungmann, "Catechumenate," p. 238.

The Fathers offer a twofold explanation of this rite: exsufflation signifying the expulsion of Satan and insufflation signifying infusion of the Holy Spirit.

Bishops of this era repeatedly insisted on the necessity of faith and, therefore, stressed the importance of serious evangelization prior to admission to baptism. Athanasius states:

> The Savior commanded not only to baptize he said first "to teach" and then "to baptize" so that teaching may give birth to the proper faith and that, with the faith we may be initiated by the sacrament. . . . Indeed, the body cannot receive the sacrament of baptism if the soul, before all else, has not welcomed the truth of the faith.[13]

The faith of which these bishops spoke was not simply an intellectual assent. Rather, in their preaching they insisted that conversion be manifested by a life conformed to the faith. John Chrysostom in a baptismal instruction states unequivocally:

> I have said it before, I say it now, and I shall say it again and again: unless a man has corrected the defects of his character and has developed a facility for virtue, let him not be baptized.[14]

At the same time, patristic sermons are replete with exhortations to catechumens not to postpone reception of the sacrament, but to present themselves as candidates for Easter baptism.

For those who presented themselves, there was an enrollment of names toward the beginning of the Lenten season. It consisted in an examination of the candidates' lives and an inscription. During the course of the rite the bishop asked witnesses who knew the catechumens to testify to their way of life. If the testimony was favorable, the candidates were chosen to be among the elect, and their names were written in the register of those to be baptized at Easter.

Lent became a period of penance and intensive instruction on the Scriptures, the Creed, and the Our Father. During

---

[13] Dujarier, *A History of the Catechumenate*, p. 86.
[14] Dujarier, *A History of the Catechumenate*, p. 88.

the season the *traditio* or handing over of the faith was celebrated. In the rite the elect were given the Apostles' Creed, the summary of the faith. A second presentation, that of the Our Father, was added later signifying the handing on to the elect of the Christian way of prayer.

The scrutinies, celebrated in previous centuries, assumed a more definite form toward the end of the fourth century. Celebrated on the Third, Fourth, and Fifth Sundays of Lent, the scrutinies were a complex of rites. They were prepared for by prayer and fasting and included an exorcism and the rite of breathing on the elect. Their primary purpose was to purify the candidates' hearts from domination by evil spirits and to confirm them on their path to baptism.

The final liturgical celebration prior to Easter baptism included the ephphetha and the *redditio symbolorum*. The ephphetha or opening of the ears was modeled on the gospel story of Jesus curing the deaf man. The *redditio* or "handing back" involved proclamation of the Creed received and learned by the elect during Lent as a statement of their faith. Sacramental initiation of candidates was celebrated at Easter after an all night vigil as in the preceding century.

Another significant development occurred during the fourth and fifth centuries. The prevailing custom prohibited the teaching of the sacred rites of the Church to the unbaptized. Consequently, the Fathers developed a series of postbaptismal catecheses, called *mystagogia,* that were designed to explain the meaning of the rites experienced at the Easter Vigil. In these instructions, which were held daily during Easter week, the Fathers made ingenious use of natural, biblical, and cultural symbolism. Through the many associations evoked by the rites, they assisted the neophytes to plumb the depths of the Christian mysteries. After the eucharistic celebration on the octave of Easter, the candidates put aside their white baptismal robes; whence, the name "Low Sunday" or "White Sunday." Selections from the mystagogical preaching of Cyril of Jerusalem, John Chrysostom, Theodore of Mopsuestia, and Ambrose of Milan have been preserved.[15]

---

[15] For a comparative study of the mystagogical catecheses of the Church Fathers, cf. Hugh M. Riley, *Christian Initiation* (Washington, D.C.: The Catholic University of America Press, Consortium Press, 1974).

Despite the quality of liturgical preaching and the adaptations introduced into the formation of catechumens during the patristic era, changing social conditions led to serious decline in the level of Christian commitment. The changed climate within the Church weakened the quality of Christian witness which led inevitably to the devitalization of the catechumenate.

The gradual dissolution of the catechumenate continued throughout the Middle Ages. In addition to the reasons already mentioned, the barbarian invasions of the early Middle Ages led to the loss of many ancient liturgical documents and resulted in a lack of historical perspective on Christian tradition.

As early as the sixth century adult baptisms had declined in the established churches. While the number of such baptisms continued to increase in the mission countries of northern and eastern Europe, the sacrament was administered quickly with little catechetical preparation. Over the centuries church leaders, among them Popes Leo the Great, Gregory the Great, and Gregory II urged reform. Gregory the Great demanded a preparation of forty days. Later, Gregory II insisted that baptism be celebrated only on the traditional feasts of Easter and Pentecost following serious preparation. Unfortunately, these reforms were often ignored.

In the case of infants there are indications that the traditional rites of the adult catechumenate were used with some adjustments. Caesar of Arles (sixth century) urged mothers not to miss the celebration of the scrutinies. These celebrations, increased to seven in number, were transferred to weekdays in Lent. The scrutinies, all that remained of the intense catechesis of previous eras, served as parental preparation for the baptism of their children. These rites and the baptismal celebration that followed represent the last vestige of Christian initiation in stages.

By the eighth century, in many places the scrutinies were collapsed into a single complicated rite. The situation continued to decline until, by the fourteenth century, rituals contained no preliminary steps to baptism.

Parallel to these developments, churches in the West increasingly reserved to the bishop the role of the postbaptismal anointing. Theologians associated this rite with the conferral of the Holy Spirit. Over the centuries these rites developed into two distinct sacraments, baptism and confirmation, with separate effects attributed to each. Moreover, reception of both sacraments was separated from first Eucharist.[16]

In the anomalous situation that developed, the prebaptismal rites that formerly spread over the course of the catechumenate were now telescoped into a single baptismal event. Whereas sacramental initiation (i.e., baptism, confirmation, and Eucharist) was so effectively separated that for centuries most Christians were not aware of any previous liturgical or theological connection.

SIGNS OF
RENEWAL

The great missionary ventures to Asia, the Americas, and Africa during the sixteenth century revived interest in the catechumenate. In their zeal to save indigenous peoples, the earliest wave of missionaries practiced mass baptisms with little catechesis preceding or following administration of the sacrament. Even so great a missionary as Francis Xavier, toward the beginning of his ministry, baptized great numbers after minimal instruction. Many subsequently abandoned the faith. In 1536 on the Fisher Coast of India alone, 10,000 people were baptized *en masse* and then left without pastoral care.[17] Similar situations existed in South America.

In the latter, the Dominicans and Augustinians began their labors to remedy the situation during the second quarter of the sixteenth century. They requested that administration of the sacrament of baptism be restricted to four feast days throughout the year: Easter, Pentecost, the feast of St. Augustine, and Epiphany. Through their efforts episcopal synods in Mexico and Peru mandated a forty-day catechumenate including prayer, fasting, and catechesis. Unfortunately, these pastoral decisions never became general practice.

Initial directives for reform in India were sent to Jesuit missionaries by Ignatius of Loyola in a letter of 1552. In it he encouraged the establishment of catechumenal communities

---

[16] For a study of the development of this phenomenon, cf. Nathan Mitchell, "Dissolution of the Rite of Christian Initiation," in *Made Not Born*, pp. 50–82.

[17] Leonel L. Mitchell, "Christian Initiation: the Reformation Period," in *Made Not Born*, p. 83.

where candidates were to come together for a period of three months.

In Europe scholars of the period were rediscovering the catechumenate. In 1602 Cardinal Sanctorius published the *Restored Roman Ritual Based on the Practice of the Ancient Church*. It contained a seven-stage rite based on the ancient catechumenate. The Ritual was never promulgated.

Drawing upon this work, the Carmelite Thomas of Jesus wrote *The Manner of Procuring Salvation For All Pagans* (1613). In it he provided catechetical content and promoted the restoration of the ancient discipline. The newly founded Propagation of the Faith distributed copies of this work to all missionaries departing for Asia.

Renewed efforts to restore adequate baptismal preparation were spearheaded in Africa by the Capuchins and the Holy Ghost missionaries in the eighteenth century. However, the renewal of the catechumenate was due largely to the vision of Cardinal Lavigerie, founder of the White Fathers, who called for the reestablishment of the catechumenate in the missions of his congregation. His catechetical system respected the stages of development of faith. Each stage of preparation for baptism was to be marked by progress in catechesis and conversion. Those who did not evidence perseverance in living their faith during the catechumenal period were not to be baptized. Cardinal Lavigerie's principles influenced other missionary congregations. The eventual restoration of the catechumenate owes much to his efforts.

In all of these attempts the catechumenate must be understood in the broadest sense. On the one hand, the catechetical revival of the Renaissance and Counter-Reformation periods contributed significantly to the development of catechumenates. Candidates received serious and systematic preparation for baptism over an extended period of time. On the other, there were marked differences between these modern catechumenates and their ancient counterparts. Impoverished liturgical and sacramental theology, especially in the area of the sacraments of initiation, resulted in praxis devoid of the catechetical breadth and the richly symbolic liturgical expression characteristic of earlier ages. Rather, catechetically, contemporary catechumenates were often no more than schools of religion in which candidates memorized catechisms. More-over, in accordance with the piety of the times, distribution of medals, rosary beads, and other objects of devotion filled the liturgical void.

The restoration of the catechetical-liturgical integrity of Christian initiation is the contribution of the twentieth century. The great streams of the catechetical movement, liturgical revival, and pastoral need intersected not only in mission lands, but in dechristianized areas of Europe. In response to a request from the bishops of France, on April 16, 1962, the Sacred Congregation of Rites issued a decree authorizing local ordinaries to perform the rites of initiation in seven stages over a period of time. Once again catechetical instruction was resituated in its liturgical framework, and the stages of the candidates' growth in faith and their ritualization by the Church were reintegrated.

From this brief overview of church history it can be seen that the catechumenate is not something new in the Catholic Church. In fact, it is something very old, rooted in the manner of development of the New Testament communities and in the early tradition of Christian initiation. It has been rediscovered and reclaimed in modern times not out of a sense of nostalgia or of fundamentalism, but rather out of pastoral need. The Holy Spirit has reawakened in the Church a sense of its mission to the world. Out of its efforts to respond to the gospel mandate to spread the Good News to every creature have come a growing appreciation of the nature of conversion, the stages of development of faith, and an understanding of faith not simply as a body of dogmas to be understood but as a way of living in the world.

Suggested Reading

(Chapter I)

Dujarier, Michel. "A Survey of the History of the Catechumenate." In *Becoming a Catholic Christian*. New York: William H. Sadlier, Inc., 1978.

_____. *A History of the Catechumenate, The First Six Centuries*. New York: William H. Sadlier, Inc., 1979.

Hovda, Robert, ed. *Made Not Born: New Perspectives on Christian Initiation and the Catechumenate*. Notre Dame: University of Notre Dame Press, 1976.

Kavanagh, Aidan, *The Shape of Baptism: the Rite of Christian Initiation* from the collection *Studies in the Reformed Rites of the Catholic Church*, vol. 1. New York: Pueblo Publishing Co., 1978.

Richardson, Cyril, ed. *Early Christian Fathers*. New York: Macmillan Publishing Co., 1970.

Study Guide

(for use with groups)

To develop an awareness of the catechumenate in Christian tradition.

PURPOSE

To reflect on the experience of coming to adult faith and conversion.

1. Reflect on your experience of coming to adult faith commitment. What were the milestones along the way? What was the turning point(s)? Can you think of a Scripture story that reflects your experience?

QUESTIONS FOR REFLECTION

2. What does (a) baptism (b) Eucharist mean for you?

3. From your reading of history, when was the catechumenate strongest? Why?

4. Reflecting on the history of the catechumenate, list the elements that are essential to the success of the initiation of candidates in any age.

Chapter II
Claiming Our Heritage

In restoring the catechumenate, the decree of 1962 (cf. chapter I), emphasized that initiation is a journey in successive stages, wherein the process of conversion is fostered and its transitions marked by liturgical rites. The stage was set for the Second Vatican Council's restoration of the rhythm of Christian initiation.

The restoration of the catechumenate was mandated in the first document issued by the Council on December 4, 1963, the Constitution on the Sacred Liturgy (SC). It states clearly:

> The catechumenate for adults, comprising several distinct steps, is to be restored . . . by this means the period of the catechumenate, which is intended as a time of suitable instruction, may be sanctified by sacred rites, to be celebrated at successive intervals (SC 64).[1]

Subsequent articles called for the cultural adaptation of the rites (SC 65), the revision of the rites of adult initiation (SC 66), and the reintegration of confirmation into its original context as part of the initiation process (SC 71).

Later documents added further dimensions. The Decree on the Missions (AG) traced the spiritual journey of the newcomers describing the periods and thresholds of conversion to Christ. The decree outlines the process: of proclamation of the mystery of Christ; conversion and faith, noting that conversion "should manifest itself through its social effects and be gradually developed during the time of the catechumenate" (AG 13); and finally, sacraments of Christian initiation.[2]

Further, the Constitution on the Church specified that catechumens are members of the household of God (LG 14);[3]

---

[1] Walter M. Abbot, SJ, ed., *The Documents of Vatican II,* "Constitution on the Sacred Liturgy" (SC), nos. 64–71 (New York: Guild Press, American Press, 1966).

[2] Abbot, "Decree on the Church's Missionary Activity" (AG), nos. 13–14. These paragraphs summarize key aspects of the conciliar vision of Christian initiation. Those responsible for implementing the RCIA would profit from serious reflection on these articles.

[3] Abbot, "Dogmatic Constitution on the Church" (LG), no. 14.

that is, they are already members of the Church, although they are not yet fully incorporated through the sacraments of initiation.

The primary responsibility for the formation of members in the local Church rests with the bishop. His is the task of overseeing the reestablishment of the catechumenate as well as the adaptation of the instruction of adult catechumens (CD 14).[4] Since the purpose of Christian initiation is incorporation into the People of God, the entire community of the faithful, especially sponsors, share in this responsibility (AG 14).[5]

THE RITE   The task of shaping this conciliar vision into reality was entrusted to the Sacred Congregation for Divine Worship. In response to that mandate, on the feast of Epiphany, January 6, 1972, the Congregation issued the decree *Ordinus Baptismi Adultorum,*[6] promulgating the *Rite of Christian Initiation of Adults* (RCIA).

So that the rite of initiation will be more useful for the work of the Church and for individual, parochial, and missionary circumstances, the rite is first presented in Part I of this book in its complete and usual form (nos. 36–251). This is designed for the preparation of a group of candidates, but by simple adaptation pastors can devise a form suited to one person.

Part II provides rites for special circumstances: the Christian initiation of children (nos. 252–330), a simple form of the rite for adults to be carried out in exceptional circumstances (nos. 331–369), and a short form of the rite for those in danger of death (nos. 370–399). Part II also includes guidelines for preparing uncathechized adults for confirmation and eucharist (nos. 400–410) along with four (4) optional rites which may be used with such candidates, and the rite of reception of baptized Christians into the full communion of the Catholic Church (nos. 473–504).

---

[4] Abbot, "Decree on the Bishops' Pastoral Office in the Church" (CD), no. 14.

[5] Abbot, "Decree on the Church's Missionary Activity" (AG), no. 14.

[6] Sacred Congregation for Divine Worship, *Ordo Initiationis Christianae Adultorum* (Vatican City: Vatican Press, 1972). The *Rite of Christian Initiation of Adults,* English text (Washington, D.C.: United States Catholic Conference Office of Publishing and Promotion Services, 1988.)

Rites for catechumens and baptized but previously uncat-
echized adults celebrated in combination, along with a rite
combining the reception of baptized Christians into the full
communion of the Catholic Church with the celebration of
Christian initiation at the Easter Vigil (nos. 562–594), are
contained in Appendix I. The two additional appendices con-
tain acclamations, hymns, and songs, and the National Stat-
utes for the Catechumenate in the Dioceses of the United
States of America.[7]

The first of these rites, the Rite of Christian Initiation of
Adults, is normative. It includes not only the sacraments of
initiation: baptism, confirmation, Eucharist, but the rites of
the catechumenate as well. The remaining rites cover the
pastoral needs of particular groups or individual persons. Since
that is the case, this Study Text will focus primarily on the
first rite.

The Rite of Christian Initiation of Adults presents a vision   SCOPE
of faith as a developing reality that brings the believer into
relationship with God and with all believers. It contains a
vision of the Church as a people brought together by a common
experience of conversion and faith in Jesus Christ and gifted
with the life of the Spirit through baptism. As a result, they
are incorporated into an ecclesial body committed to continuing the mission of the Lord in the world through personal and
corporate witness of lived faith.

The process and structures outlined in the RCIA are
intended for the formation of new members in all facets of
ecclesial life: Scripture, doctrine, liturgy, morality, and ministry, while gradually incorporating them into full membership. It is not designed simply as a preparation for the sacraments of initiation, but rather for a *life of faith* within the
Catholic Church.

To accomplish this end, the Church has reformed the
process through which new members are received. In the
immediate past the primary model was convert instruction
either individually or in groups. The goal of the teaching method
is the transmission of knowledge, that is, of the doctrines held

---

[7] RCIA, no 3.

by the Catholic Church. The primary aim was to teach the convert to know the faith.

In the RCIA the model is a process of initiation. The desired goal is twofold: first of all, personal commitment to Christ and therefore, to a way of life based on the Gospel; second, integration into the ecclesial community. Initiation of this nature takes place in the context of a community. Within that context there are many different roles: sponsors, godparents, catechists, guides, role models, peers, the community itself. All are responsible in varying degrees for the formation of new members.

It is not surprising that the Catholic Church, at this transitional point in its existence, would rediscover the importance of Christian initiation. Turning points in the lives of groups, as in the lives of individuals, weaken the sense of identity and affect deeply the unity and cohesiveness of the group. In the Church universal, through the active participation of its members, a renewed identity is being shaped and integrated.

It is in this postconciliar pastoral context that the Church has opted for initiation as the method of forming new members. Its purpose is the creation of a strong sense of *personal Christian identity* and *communal solidarity*. On the one hand, through it the faith of the candidate is shaped and his/her conversion deepened by and within the believing community. On the other, through the participation of the faithful in the catechumenal process, the community continually renews its own faith and growth by giving birth to new generations of believers.

In the words of the rite:

> The initiation of catechumens is a gradual process that takes place within the community of the faithful. By joining the catechumens in reflecting on the value of the paschal mystery and by renewing their own conversion, the faithful provide an example that will help the catechumens to obey the Holy Spirit more generously (RCIA 4).

This paragraph highlights not only the communal nature of initiation, but also the core of Christian faith and the importance of time in the conversion process.

The central mystery of faith is the paschal mystery. The death-resurrection of Jesus contains within itself the very meaning of Christian discipleship. In its light Christians answer symbolically the great questions of human existence: who God is; the meaning of suffering, of life, of death. It is *the mystery of faith,* that which we believe, celebrate, and live in the world and into which we initiate new members. It is the paradigm of Christian spirituality as well as of Christian life styles. Those involved in Christian formation have a particular responsibility to continually deepen their understanding of the paschal mystery as revealed in the Scriptures, celebrated in the worship of the Church, and expressed in the lived vocation of Christians to be salt, leaven, and light in the world.[8]

The RCIA respects the developmental phases of faith and conversion. The catechumenate is not a program but a gradual process in which adults hear "the mystery of Christ proclaimed, consciously and freely seek the living God and enter the way of faith and conversion as the Holy Spirit opens their hearts" (RCIA 1). What the rite is calling for is personal response to the gift of the Spirit. While the communication of the faith of the Church may involve programmed aspects, it is important to remember that a qualitative personal response in the faith can never be programmed. The rite is permeated with language that draws attention to the "gradual process" of development of faith and therefore, of initiation into the Church. It speaks of periods, or progressive stages and steps; of new beginnings, of a journey; of crossroads and transitions; of guides and companions on the way that leads to adult ecclesial conversion. In other words, the rite envisions a journey of faith leading to full incorporation into the community of the faithful.

It is important to note the terminology of the rite. The introduction refers to three steps (RCIA 6). These steps are not to be confused with the periods of the catechumenate. Rather, as the rite indicates, they are "steps" or "doorways," that is, the transition points between each of the periods of the catechumenate. Each step is marked by a liturgical rite the purpose of which is to celebrate what occurred in the

OVERVIEW OF THE RITE

---

[8] For a presentation of the paschal mystery on a popular level, cf. Barbara O'Dea, DW, *Of Fast and Festival* (New York/Ramsey: Paulist Press, 1982).

previous period and to mandate and strengthen the candidates for the period ahead.

Step 1   The first step of the rite is the passage into the catechumenate. It takes place at the point of initial conversion when inquirers have decided that they wish to become Christians. Having decided on their readiness for this step, the Church for its part receives them as catechumens (RCIA 6, 1). The Rite of Acceptance into the Order of Catechumens celebrates the first step of Christian initiation, entrance into the order of catechumens. Through it inquirers become members of the household of the faith (LG 14).

Step 2   The second step or transition is the admission of candidates to a period of intense preparation for the sacraments of initiation. It takes place when faith has matured and the period of catechumenal formation is drawing to a close. At this point the catechumen must request admission to the Easter sacraments. The Church once again judges their readiness and decides on their admission to the following period. The Rite of Election or Enrollment of Names is the second major celebration or step of the RCIA. Through it catechumens become the elect, those chosen for Easter baptism (RCIA 6, 2).

Step 3   The third step of the rite is the celebration of the sacraments of initiation. It takes place after the period of immediate preparation. The celebration of the sacraments of initiation (i.e., the sacraments of baptism, confirmation, and Eucharist) marks this final celebration of the Rite of Christian Initiation of Adults. Through it candidates become full members of the ecclesial body (RCIA 6, 3).

OVERVIEW OF THE PERIODS   The rite notes four periods in the initiation process. Their purpose is initial inquiry into the faith of the Church and subsequent development of faith and conversion.

First Period   The first period involves inquiry on the part of the candidates and initial evangelization and the precatechumenate on the part of the Church (RCIA 7, 1). There is no particular time span assigned to this period. It begins when the candidate presents him/herself. Its length is determined by the needs and readiness of the person involved.

This period opens with the liturgical celebration of acceptance into the order of catechumens. The purpose of the catechumenate is the education and maturing of the catechumen's faith. Through its various ministers the Church provides catechesis and celebrates rites that provide opportunities for the candidates to internalize the faith of the Church. This period may last several years; however, the length of the catechumenate is flexible. It is to be determined not by the calendar, but by the needs of the catechumens (RCIA 7, 2).

Ordinarily the third period, known as the period of purification and enlightenment, coincides with the season of Lent. During this period of immediate preparation for the Easter celebration of the sacraments of initiation, the candidates devote themselves in a more intense way to personal asceticism and prayer. In this manner they continue to purify their motivation and deepen their commitment to Christ. The prayer of the Church heals, strengthens, and supports them on the way, particularly through the Lenten rites of the catechumenate (RCIA 7, 3; 8).

The period of postbaptismal catechesis or mystagogy period is the final period of incorporation of new members into the ecclesial body. Ordinarily, this period extends through the whole Easter season. An intense experience of the sacramental and communal life of the Church characterizes this time during which the unity of the faithful is celebrated and deepened (RCIA 7, 4; 8).

The overview of the Rite of Christian Initiation of Adults, contained in its introductory paragraphs, concludes with an important principle:

> The whole initiation must bear a markedly paschal character, since the initiation of Christians is the first sacramental sharing in Christ's dying and rising and since, in addition, the period of purification and enlightenment ordinarily coincides with Lent[2] and the period of postbaptismal catechesis or mystagogy with the Easter season (RCIA 8).

It is to assume this paschal focus that the final periods of initiation coincide with Lent and Eastertime. Although the rite allows for the celebration of the sacraments of initiation outside the context of the Easter Vigil in the case of pastoral need, this remains the exception. Pastoral leaders who understand the meaning of Christian initiation and the rhythm of the church year will use this option in response to situations of genuine need.

Step/ Doorway	Period	Role of Church	Task of Candidate	Length
Rite of Acceptance into the Order of Catechumens	Evangelization and Pre-catechumenate	Welcome; Initial proclamation of the Gospel; Decision to admit to membership	Initial faith and conversion; Decision to seek membership in the Church	Not specified
Rite of Election or Enrollment of Names	Catechumenate	Complete catechesis; Affirmation and support; Decision to admit to Sacraments of Initiation	Maturing of faith and conversion; Deepening commitment to Christ demonstrated in life style; Gradual integration into the Church; Decision to receive baptism	Flexible up to three years
Celebration of the Sacraments of Initiation	Purification and Enlightenment	Parish Lenten observance; scrutinies, presentations; preparation of candidates for Sacraments of Initiation	Intense spiritual preparation for Sacraments of Initiation	Lenten season (Ash Wednesday– Holy Thursday)
	Postbaptismal Catechesis or Mystagogy	Postbaptismal catechesis, especially through the Sunday eucharistic celebrations	Deepening Christian experience; full integration into the community of the faithful	Easter season (Easter– Pentecost)

Suggested Reading

(Chapter II)

BOOKS   Dujarier, Michel. *The Rites of Christian Initiation: Historical and Pastoral Reflections.* New York: William H. Sadlier, Inc., 1979.

Dunning, James B. *New Wine: New Wineskins.* Exploring the RCIA. New York: William H. Sadlier, Inc., 1981.

Kemp, Raymond B. *A Journey in Faith, An Experience of the Catechumenate.* New York: William H. Sadlier, Inc., 1979.

Lewinski, Ronald. *Welcoming the New Catholic. An Introduction to the Rite of Christian Initiation of Adults.* Chicago: Liturgy Training Program, 1978.

Sacred Congregation for Divine Worship, *Rite of Christian Initiation of Adults.* Washington, D.C.: United States Catholic Conference Office of Publishing and Promotion Services, 1988.

ARTICLES   Beraudy, Roger. "The New Ritual for Adult Baptism." In *Theology Digest* 24:1 (Spring 1976): 57–62.

Hanson, Donald M. "The Rite of Christian Initiation: An Introduction." In *Christian Initiation Resources* 1:1, pp. 7–13.

Kavanagh, Aidan, OSB. "Christian Initiation of Adults: The Rites." In *Worship,* vol. 48 (1974): 318–335.

Study Guide

(for use with groups)

PURPOSE   To reflect on the process of initiation as presented in the RCIA.

To raise the awareness of Catholic parishioners of foundational dimensions of the faith into which we initiate new members.

1. The paschal mystery in an *event:* the death-resurrection of Jesus which forms the *paradigm* or pattern of Christian life and spirituality.

Recall an experience in your life where you recognize this pattern of letting go in order to reach out to growth and new life.

2. Nurturing the seeds of conversion and faith is the purpose of the catechumenate. How can the pace of conversion in individual candidates be respected?

How might the programmatic aspects of the parish catechumenate be made sufficiently flexible to allow for different patterns of response and readiness?

3. Whom do you consider to be a person who exemplifies a true Christian life? How is it manifested? What does the way this person lives reveal about what he or she truly believes?

4. How can the parish catechumenate be planned to foster a *life of faith?*

5. How might those responsible for the parish catechumenate assist candidates to develop a sense of belonging to the parish? to the local Church? to the universal Church?

Chapter III

Evangelization and Precatechumenate
(RCIA 36-43)

Period	Role of Church	Task of Candidate	Length
Evangelization and Precatechumenate	Welcome; Initial proclamation of the Gospel; Decision to admit to membership	Initial faith and conversion; Decision to seek membership in the Church	Not specified

The precatechumenate or inquiry period, although a preliminary period, is of utmost importance. It is the time during which the candidate and the Christian community establish communication. According to the rite, on the part of the Church, "[i]t is a time of evangelization: faithfully and constantly the living God is proclaimed and Jesus Christ whom he has sent for the salvation of all" (RCIA 36).

It is important to note from the beginning that the entire Rite of Christian Initiation is designed primarily for inquirers "who are not yet Christians" (RCIA 36). In the United States some of those who express interest in becoming Catholic Christians have never been evangelized, others trace their journey of faith through contact with and even baptism in other Christian churches. In such cases, ecumenical sensitivity and respect for prior Christian baptism must be practiced.

While it is helpful to include persons baptized in other churches in a process of incorporation into the Catholic Church, it is important to adapt the process to their situation. It must be remembered that for them it is not a question of coming to initial faith in God or in Jesus Christ, but of deepening their faith and conversion and of identification with and incorporation into full membership in the Catholic Church. The criterion for determining whether or not a candidate for reception into full communion should embark on a catechumenal experience consists in the discernment of adult conversion. To what extent has the prospective candidate appropriated the gospel message in his/her life? Dialogue with the inquirer will enlighten the pastoral staff on whether or not a period of extended conversion is appropriate. All baptized candidates should be exposed to an introduction to the Catholic way of life, to a Lenten experience of immediate spiritual preparation, and to an Easter reflection on the effects of their baptism—confirmation and Eucharist.

WELCOMING INQUIRERS

Determination of the needs of candidates is a first step in designing the inquiry experience. Even as those responsible plan the precatechumenate, the parish welcomes the inquirers. For the faithful, this is a time to reach out to those who have manifested a desire to know the faith of the Church. Hospitality, which should be the hallmark of the parish community throughout the initiation process, is crucial during the initial period. The witness of welcome and hospitality sets the tone for the entire process. It contributes to the creation of a climate of trust and facilitates a sense of belonging. This atmosphere is important in assisting newcomers to feel comfortable with members of the community, free to interact with them and to participate actively in the process of evangelization. A parish that knows how to welcome inquirers with warmth, interest, and hospitality is itself a catalyst in the evangelization process. Through their witness, members contribute greatly to the identification of newcomers with the Church.

For inquirers the precatechumenate is a time of identification and inclusion, a time to get to know the faith and the faithful on a less formal basis than in the following periods. In relation to the Church the movement of inquirers is from *we/they* to *us*. In this initial period, informal gatherings can be arranged so that candidates meet various people and groups in the parish (e.g., the parish council, parish sponsors, a bible study group). While these occasions may be primarily social, provision should be made for meaningful introductions including some introduction to the role of the person or group in the parish. These gatherings may take place at the parish or may be held in the homes of various parishioners.

Such occasions are important not only for inquirers. If initiation is to "take place within the community of the faithful" (RCIA 4), parishioners must get to know who the inquirers are, so that they may begin to accompany and support them on their journey of faith.[1] The interaction of inquirers and parishioners offers the latter the opportunity to exercise their Christian vocation and to be renewed by the witness of inquirers. Often it is in sharing with newcomers that Catholic parishioners discover that as Church we do have Good News to share.

These meetings will help inquirers to develop a sense of relatedness to the parish. Through such informal gatherings they discover groups with similar interests (e.g., choirs, prayer groups, social action committees) which open up opportunities for further integration into the parish. The role of these informal gatherings, for both inquirers and the parish community, should not be underestimated.

For those who bear a particular responsibility for the inquiry period—catechists, sponsors, deacons, priests—the pre-catechumenate is a time to promote contacts with the parish community and to become personally acquainted with the inquirers in order to provide an explanation of the Gospels adapted to them (RCIA 38).

PERSONAL ACQUAINTANCE

Not to be underestimated in the process of getting to know the candidates is the role of interviewing. Once the inquirer has expressed interest, personal contact should be arranged in a comfortable setting (perhaps the candidate's home). Care should be taken to assure that persons designated by the parish to conduct these interviews have the ability to set people at ease, to listen actively, and to enter into dialogue comfortably.

The purpose of the initial interview is to discover what led the person to the point of inquiry, some basic personal background, and any particular questions or difficulties that will need to be addressed.

If the interview reveals situations such as divorce and remarriage, it is important to start early to deal with them in order to avoid difficulties later in the process. Diocesan marriage tribunals are prepared to be helpful with cases of prospective catechumens and candidates for full reception. Those implementing the parish catechumenate should be encouraged

---

[1] For a practical development of this point, cf. Raymond B. Kemp, "First Stage: The Precatechumenate," *A Journey in Faith*, pp. 31–64.

to establish a working relationship with the tribunal, so that the needs of a prospective catechumen might be met early in the process and an appropriate period of time be allowed for healing before or as the conversion process of the catechumenate proper begins.

EVANGELIZATION

Inclusion of inquirers by members of the parish is for a purpose. On the part of the Church the primary purpose of the inquiry period is evangelization. Faith and initial conversion are the desired response (RCIA 37). Conversion is not an option, but a gospel imperative. To "repent and believe the Good News" (Mk 1:15) is the first step in becoming a Christian of mature faith. A climate of welcome puts inquirers at ease and disposes them to enter into the evangelization process with open hearts and trusting spirits.

In 1974 the Synod of Bishops defined evangelization as "the activity whereby the Church proclaims the Gospel so that faith may be aroused, may unfold and may grow."[2] The RCIA describes the desired response to goals of evangelization in the inquiry stage as faith, initial conversion, and commitment to Christ (RCIA 36, 37). From this it is obvious that inquirers are not students gathered to learn a body of knowledge. Rather, they are disciples in the process of discovering a way of life.[3]

Evangelization assumes God's call and presence in the life of the inquirer. Through proclamation of the Gospel the Church calls forth a response. To elicit this personal response evangelization must be grounded in human experience. The mystery of God's presence is to be discovered within the life experience of the inquirers. Therefore, they should be assisted to focus attention on the stepping stones, transitions, and transformations that have taken place in their lives. Therein, they will discover the path along which God is leading them. The dynamic is dialogue between personal history and the gospel story. There must be a time for speaking and a time for listening, so that the inquirer may gradually discover in the

---

[2] *The Evangelization of the Modern World,* Synod of Bishops (Washington, D.C.: United States Catholic Conference Office of Publishing and Promotion Services, 1973), p. 2.

[3] Cf. Andre Aubry's distinction between a "school" and an "initiation" in "Pastoral Dimensions of the Adult Rite of Initiation," *Christian and Parish Rebirth and Renewal* (Washington, D.C.: Federation of Diocesan Liturgical Commissions [FDLC], 1976).

paradigm and rhythm of the Gospels, the meaning of his/her own life experience.

This implies that evangelizers—catechist, priest, or faithful—must be aware of the centrality of the paschal mystery in order to respect the "strong paschal character" of the whole initiation process.[4] The Good News is that God sent his Son for the salvation of the world. Everything in the Gospel, all the words and the works of Jesus throughout his ministry, draw his hearers to conversion, faith, and living the values of the Kingdom of God here and now. His final exodus through death to life proclaims the ultimate victory.

In the process of evangelization inquirers are to reinterpret their life story in the light of the Gospel. It is there that they are to discover God's call to conversion and faith; his desire to forgive and heal along with the hope that in and through personal struggles, doubts, trials, new life and growth will come forth. In other words, it is in dialogue with the Gospels that inquirers will discover that their life experience takes on meaning and direction in the light of the paschal mystery. This discovery leads to initial conversion and commitment to Christ.

Moreover, the goal of evangelization is not simply dialogue between personal experience and the Gospels. Catechists must be attentive to the corporate dimension of the Christian call. It is together that Christians are the Body of Christ; together that we are called to be salt to the earth and light to the world. The call of God and the paschal dimension of the Church's story, as presented in Scripture and tradition, must be communicated, so that candidates may come to recognize in the Church the Body of Christ in which the life of the Spirit and the mission to spread the Good News continues. This "allows for the discovery of *Church* as a people who find their identity in the paschal mystery and who continue the pattern in their lives."[5] The outcome will be a growing sense of relatedness to the Catholic Church. Evangelization roots

---

[4] The paschal mystery, Jesus' death-resurrection, is the central event in salvation history. The pattern underlying all of Christian initiation involves *dying* to all that is not of Christ and *rising* to new life in him.

[5] For a development of the role of storytelling and questioning in Christian initiation, cf. James B. Dunning, "The Stages of Initiation: Part 1. Inquiry," in *Becoming a Catholic Christian* (New York: William H. Sadlier, Inc., 1978), pp. 91–103.

chesis that is to follow in the Gospels and in life, the personal-communal lives of Catholic Christians.

As presented above, this initial evangelization is intended to introduce inquirers into the heart of the gospel message. It presents an overview of the Good News constantly in relation to the formative event that gives meaning to the whole; the paschal mystery. It sets the dialogue between inquirer, Gospel, and Church in motion.

While it is important that both church ministers and candidates have an initial grasp of the scope of the vision during this period, those working with inquirers must keep in mind that it is indeed an initial period. People come with a variety of motives ranging from the superficial to the profound. It is the role of evangelizers to lead inquirers to reflect on what motivates their search. Gospel insights, reflection on personal and Church experience, questions raised during this period will continue to be pursued, explored, and illuminated throughout the initiation process. Letting go of anything blatantly sinful, and reaching out to the Gospel as the way to life in Christ along with a certain sense of Church (RCIA 41, 42), is the basic task of inquirers during the precatechumenate.

READINESS TO
BECOME
CATECHUMENS

Readiness to move to the first step of the rite is based on several criteria: evidence of initial faith and conversion, desire to follow Christ, and intention to seek baptism (RCIA 37, 42).

The first step of the rite is the acceptance into the order of catechumens. Since catechumens are already members of the Church, in order to take this step, candidates must have made decisions regarding two matters. The first of these is discipleship. According to the rite, there must be a manifest desire to follow Christ. The purpose of evangelization is to educate that initial attraction until desire increases to the point where the candidates wish to make the Gospel the pattern of their lives. That implies a willingness to "take up one's cross and follow," to experience the pain as well as the glory of discipleship, and a dawning awareness that the presence and action of God can be discovered in both dimensions.

Second, the desire to seek baptism must be present. The goal of initiation is incorporation into the Body of Christ. This takes place through the sacraments of initiation in which believers are baptized into the dying and rising of Christ and incorporated into the body of the faithful. Candidates for the catechumenate must have the desire eventually to become full members of the Church through baptism. Such readiness must not be assumed. It is the responsibility of pastors, in collaboration with catechists and others involved with inquirers, to evaluate readiness for this step. Moreover, time should be set aside to ascertain candidates' reasons for requesting to become catechumens and, where needed, to give personal attention to those who need to clarify or purify their motives (RCIA 43).

It is advisable, whenever possible, to allow time between the final meeting of the inquirers and the celebration of the Rite of Acceptance into the Order of Catechumens. This encourages a decision on the part of inquirers and allows the opportunity for pastors or their delegates to interview candidates and work with them. Readiness cannot be programmed. It is preferable that individuals who feel they are not ready postpone reception as catechumens. This does not indicate that they may not continue their catechetical formation. It simply shows respect for God's action in their lives and the pace of their personal journey of faith.

The role of prayer during the precatechumenate period is not spelled out. The rite simply indicates that ". . . parish priests (pastors) should help those taking part in it with prayers suited to them . . ." (RCIA 40). It is important that those involved in ministry to inquirers—pastors, catechists, deacons, groups of parishioners—integrate prayer into the inquiry experience. Prayer is an essential catalyst in the dialogue between personal experience and the call of God. The message of the Gospel cannot be internalized without it. The integration of prayer involves the encouragement of personal prayer, teaching of traditional prayers, and an initial experience of praying with others which evolves from sharing the gospel message. Pastors are responsible for seeing that prayer is encouraged and experiences provided. They may see to it personally or through others. In either case, the experience of prayer should be integral to the precatechumenate and must continue throughout the initiation process.

A final consideration, with regard to the precatechumenate period, has to do with the provision for some type of formalized reception for interested inquirers by episcopal conferences (RCIA 39). While the bishops' conference has not considered a formalized reception necessary in our country, the reasons for this paragraph must not be overlooked. The local Church must see to it that the legitimate needs of inquirers are met in other ways. For instance, in cases where the precatechumenate has been delayed for any reason, a gesture of outreach and welcome by the Catholic community is both appropriate and desirable. Parishes can and should provide opportunities for the inquirer to be introduced by a friend to a priest as well as to other members of the community.

CONCLUSION   It should be clear that the precatechumenate is an initial, but not optional, period of the initiation process. The welcome and inclusion into the community of believers are essential to a sense of relatedness and a desire for membership in the Church. In this context evangelization can take place, and a response of faith and initial conversion is encouraged. It is crucial that those responsible for the catechumenate in the parish take pains to create the climate and provide opportunities that encourage openness to the Spirit and commitment to Christ in the Church.

Suggested Reading

(Chapter III)

The Rite of Christian Initiation of Adults, nos. 36–43.

Bohr, David. "Evangelization, Conversion and the RCIA." In *Christian Initiation Resources* (Spring 1981):259–263.

Dunning, James B. "The Stages of Initiation: Part 1. Inquiry." In *Becoming a Catholic Christian,* pp. 91–103. New York: William H. Sadlier, Inc., 1978.

Kemp, Raymond B. "First Stage: The Pre-catechumenate." In *A Journey in Faith,* pp. 31–64. New York: William H. Sadlier, Inc., 1979.

Study Guide

(for use with groups)

To develop an understanding of the precatechumenate.

To explore the role of the parish community and the task of the inquirer during this initial period.

1. How would you explain the purpose of the precatechumenate to:
    a. other parishioners?
    b. a neighbor who seems interested in becoming a Catholic Christian?

2. How does the parish discern the background in faith and the needs of:
    a. inquirers who are unbaptized?
    b. Christians baptized in another communion who seek admission to the Catholic Church?

What changes, if any, would you suggest in this approach?

3. What opportunities are provided for inquirers to meet with parishioners? How is dialogue among them facilitated?

4. How is evangelization carried out in the precatechumenate? In what ways are inquirers helped to reflect on their lives, in light of the Scriptures?

5. Who are the other people and/or groups in the parish whose participation might be a valuable contribution to the accomplishment of the goals of the precatechumenate? How?

Chapter IV

The Catechumenate
(RCIA 9, 2; 16; 41-105; 147–148; 157)

Step/ Doorway	Period	Role of Church	Task of Candidate	Length
Rite of Acceptance into the Order of Catechumens	Catechumenate	Complete catechesis; Affirmation and support; Decision to admit to Sacraments of Initiation	Maturing of faith and conversion; Deepening commitment to Christ demonstrated in life style; Gradual integration into the Church; Decision to receive baptism	Flexible up to three years

Sufficient time should be set aside between the inquiry period and the catechumenate to allow for adequate preparation for this important step (RCIA 43). During this time, pastors evaluate the external indications of readiness of the candidate with the help of sponsors, catechists, and deacons (RCIA 43), and with the candidates themselves. Where motivation is confused or decision weak, candidates can be helped to clarify their motives and strengthen their resolve. The break between the two periods is a safeguard against assumptions on the part of either those working with inquirers or of the candidates themselves. *It must not be assumed* that all inquirers either desire to or are ready to become catechumens. In meetings of the members of the catechumenal team and in personal interviews between priests and candidates, desire, motivation, and readiness should be the focus of discussion as well as any doubts, questions, or difficulties the candidate may be experiencing.

Besides the questions of motivation, other signs of readiness for this step indicated in the rite include:

- evidence of first faith, that is, of the beginnings of spiritual life and a grasp of the fundamentals of Christian teachings;
- signs of initial conversion and the desire to change one's life;
- evidence of the first stirrings of repentance;
- desire to enter into a relationship with God in Christ;
- calling on God in prayer;
- some experience of the company and spirit of Christians;
- previous contact with a priest or some member of the community;
- preparation of the candidate for the Rite of Acceptance into the Order of Catechumens (RCIA 41, 42).

During the course of interviews, options should be made clear to candidates. They may ask for admission to the catechumenate, continue as inquirers, or, having completed their inquiry, terminate the experience. Those who are not ready to take this step, can be invited to attend the liturgical celebration and to continue the programmatic aspects of the catechumenate. They can be formally incorporated when they are ready to make that decision. *Sometimes the best decision is to wait.*

In addition, pastors must be sure that baptized persons, in their eagerness for a new beginning in their lives, do not seek to be rebaptized (RCIA 43). Although this may appear self-evident, experience demonstrates that at times candidates baptized as infants into other Christian communions or even into the Catholic Church, at the moment of internalizing their commitment through a personal experience of faith and conversion, desire to repeat the sacrament. Pastors must gently but firmly explain the nature of baptism and instruct the candidate in the path open to him/her in the journey to full communion in the Catholic Church (cf. chapter VIII).

The Rite
(RCIA 48-68)

The Rite of Acceptance into the Order of Catechumens marks the entrance of candidates into the order of catechumens. Assembled publicly for the first time, they manifest their desires and make their intentions known to the Church. The celebrant and the assembled faithful pray over the candidates and in the name of the whole Church admit those who intend to become members and consecrate them to Christ through the sign of the cross (RCIA 41, 44, 45).

Participation of the faithful is not optional. The RCIA clearly mandates that "At the celebrations belonging to the period of the catechumenate, the faithful should seek to be present whenever possible and should take an active part in the responses, prayers, singing, and acclamations" (RCIA 9, 2). They represent the Church who "carrying out its apostolic mission, accepts them as persons who intend to become its members. God showers his grace on the candidates, since the celebration manifests their desire publicly and marks their reception and first consecration by the Church" (RCIA 41). The best time for this rite is within the major Sunday eucharistic celebration. Appropriate preparation of the parish assembly is clearly indicated, since at this celebration the parish community accepts responsibility for the catechumens' education in the faith in the fullest sense of that term. The rite assumes a parish ready to welcome candidates and to journey with them, thereby exercising its apostolic mandate to spread the Good News and make disciples. The celebration of the Rite of Acceptance into the Order of Catechumens launches both the candidates and the parish into a new period of growth in faith.

The Rite of Acceptance into the Order of Catechumens consists of the presentation of candidates, the Liturgy of the Word, and the dismissal of the catechumens.

Receiving the Candidates

As the rite is about to begin, candidates assemble at the entrance to the church (RCIA 48). After an initial instruction by the celebrant (RCIA 49), there is an opening dialogue with the candidates centering on what they are asking of the Church. Answers to the celebrant's questions may be expressed in the candidates' own words (RCIA 50). If this introductory dialogue is to be personalized, preparation is important to assist candidates in reflecting upon and formulating their requests. The celebrant should adapt the questions to the candidates' responses. The ritual celebration is greatly enhanced by this personal involvement. During this dialogue, and indeed throughout the entire celebration, attention should be given and the rite choreographed to ensure the *visibility* and *audibility* of candidates.

Where pastorally desirable, a rite of exorcism and a renunciation of non-Christian worship follow. While the latter are not to be systematically excluded in an age where cults and sects abound, they are not always appropriate. A pastoral judgment must be made. In any case, if candidates are from a Christian background, all references to pagan religions as well as the forswearing of false religions should be omitted.

After the dialogue, the celebrant addresses the candidates and invites them to accept publicly the Gospel for the first time (RCIA 52). In response, the sponsors and the entire assembly are invited to affirm their willingness to support and assist the candidates to find and follow Christ (RCIA 53).

The signing of the forehead and senses which follows, signifies a claiming of the candidates for Christ. Where there are only a few candidates, signing is done by the celebrant. Signing by catechists or sponsors follows. Where the number of candidates is large, the celebrant may make the sign of the cross over all the assembled candidates, as catechists or sponsors sign them individually. While the signing of the forehead is integral to the rite, the signing of the senses, which follows, may be omitted in whole or in part, as the celebrant judges appropriate (RCIA 54–56).

The candidates are then welcomed into the Church and invited to the table of God's Word. At this point, the celebrant leads the newly accepted catechumens and their sponsors into the body of the Church (RCIA 60).

Liturgy of the Word

The Scriptures are the source of spiritual nourishment of the candidates during the entire period of the catechumenate. During the Liturgy of the Word, the Lectionary or Bible should be honored in a special way. The book itself, made of worthy materials, should be carried in solemn procession, and incensed as it is placed on the lectern (RCIA 61).

After the proclamation of the Gospel and the homily, the celebrant may present the catechumens with an appropriate symbol of the Christian faith into which they are being initiated: a book of the Gospels, or a cross (RCIA 64).

The catechumens are then dismissed (RCIA 67). The celebration of the Eucharist follows. While the dismissal is difficult for the American mentality to accept, it can be a powerful witness. If properly done, the rite will not be a demonstration of the exclusion of catechumens by an elitist assembly. Nor is it the dispersion of the candidates. Rather, they are sent forth, accompanied by some of the faithful, to continue their formation through reflection on the Word of God as presented in the liturgy or on their experience of the Rite of Acceptance into the Order of Catechumens. Thus, they are enriched by the sharing of their "joy and spiritual experiences" (RCIA 67A). Those who lead them in this sharing should be formed for their ministry.

Dismissal

After the celebration of the rite, the names of the candidates are to be inscribed in the register of catechumens. The names of the celebrant and sponsors, along with the date and place, should be included (RCIA 46). Since this is not the Rite of Election celebrating the admission to baptism at the beginning of Lent, the names are not to be written during the ceremony. In addition to its baptismal register, the parish should have a register of catechumens for this inscription.

The catechumens are now members of the Church with the rights and privileges that membership in the order of catechumens brings (RCIA 47).

THE CATECHUMENATE

The catechumenate will be for them a prolonged period of pastoral formation (RCIA 75), which has for its purpose the deepening of conversion to a new way of life in Christ gradually assimilated and lived for the rest of their lives. During this period, candidates are instructed in all aspects of Christian life, initiated into the mysteries of salvation and into the practice of a gospel way of life, and enriched by the liturgical rites of the catechumenate.

The length of the catechumenate varies according to the circumstances of the catechumen and the local Church (RCIA 76). It is to be a sufficiently long probation for conversion and faith to mature. This may take several years, especially for those with no previous contact with the Christian faith.

During the catechumenate, the local Church assumes the responsibility of nourishing the catechumens with the Word

Role of the Church

of God and helping them by appropriate liturgical celebrations (RCIA 47).

In addition, so that the "dispositions manifested at their acceptance into the catechumenate are brought to maturity . . . candidates are given suitable pastoral formation and guidance, aimed at training them in the Christian life" (RCIA 75).

This is achieved through:

- a gradual formation accommodated to the liturgical year and enriched by celebration of the Word;
- the example and support of sponsors, godparents, and the whole community of the faithful;
- liturgical rites;
- involvement in church ministries (RCIA 75, 78).

Gradual Formation

It is the role of the catechist—lay, priest, or deacon—to enlighten the faith of the catechumen. Catechesis is neither to be confused with nor reduced to instruction. Besides the knowledge component involved in the presentation of the "whole Catholic teaching," attention must also be given to the affective dimension, which fosters relationship with God and brings commitment to gospel living.

Catechumens must be helped to reflect systematically on their personal experiences in light of the Scriptures, the faith stories of disciples throughout Christian tradition, and those of contemporary Christians. Through this dialogue they will come to recognize the paradigm of the paschal mystery, not only in the life experiences of Christians throughout the ages, but in their own as well. Thus, faith becomes, not simply a body of doctrines, but a lived reality.

Reflection and discussion are important moments for assimilation of the content of the sessions, for clarification and sharing of insights and faith. Internalization is fostered by celebrations of the Word. Such catechesis will nurture a life style in accordance with the spirit of Christ. Thus, it will inspire involvement in church ministries and in its apostolic witness.

Catechesis, then, is to be both rooted in experience and experimental itself. Along with the knowledge of the mysteries of salvation, candidates are to be offered concrete experiences of community, prayer, and service. This demands planning, coordination, and the involvement of many people and groups in the parish.

Much depends on the quality of the faith community that catechizes. From among them are drawn catechists and sponsors. In their midst, the catechumens celebrate weekly the Liturgy of the Word.

Example and Support of the Community

The ministry of sponsors is of particular importance. It involves the personal support of the catechumen through stages of doubt/joy, anxiety/confidence, desire/fear that may arise in the journey of faith. Wise choice of sponsors is a key to the success of the catechumenate. The pastor with the catechumenal team is best equipped to make a suitable choice of a parishioner who might serve as a sponsor for each catechumen.

In meetings with catechumens, members of the faithful, sponsors, and others should be present to accompany the catechumens in their faith journey and to witness to and grow in their own.

Liturgical rites during the catechumenate are varied. The rite speaks of celebrations of the Word, minor exorcisms, blessings, anointing of the catechumens, and the possibility of anticipating the presentations that normally take place during Lent.

Liturgical Rites

Celebrations of the Word are integral to the formation of catechumens in Christian spirituality and in the correlation of the process with the liturgical year (RCIA 81).

Celebrations of the Word (RCIA 100, 106-108)

If these celebrations are adapted to the needs of the gathered community as intended by the rite, catechumens will gradually learn to listen to, reflect on, and allow their prayer and their response to be shaped by the Word of God.

The rite mentions two moments when the Word of God is to be celebrated. The first is the Sunday celebration, which serves the double purpose of sanctifying the Lord's day (RCIA 83) and inserting the catechumens into the community of the faithful. For some catechumens, participation in the Liturgy of the Word may be a relatively recent experience; others may have celebrated it over a long period of time. In either case, the liturgical structure of this rite and the meaning of the Scriptures must be gradually opened up to them.

Before dismissing the catechumens, it is appropriate to invite them to ponder the Word of God and to have the assembly pray for them. In addition, the presiding minister may lay hands on the candidates. The profession of faith and the general intercessions follow immediately on the dismissal.

After the dismissal, the catechumens are gathered for continued reflection on the Word of God, especially the Gospels, proclaimed in the assembly. The purpose of this reflection is to allow the catechumens to experience the Word as a two-edged sword, which furthers their personal and communal conversion. In parishes where all catechesis is offered at this time, this shared reflection should last longer than the end of the Mass from which they have been excused.

Second, celebrations of God's Word may be held at the closing of catechetical sessions. This allows time for internalization of what has taken place during the session. In the words of the rite, these celebrations are "to implant in their hearts the teachings they are receiving: for example, the morality characteristic of the New Testament, the forgiving of injuries and insults, a sense of sin and repentance, the duties Christians must carry out in the world . . ." (RCIA 82, 1).

In addition, celebrations of the Word provide opportunities for relation of catechesis to the church year and for the formation of candidates in prayer and liturgical spirituality. Moreover, they provide the occasion to experience and reflect on the symbols and seasons of the liturgy with the catechumens, thus gradually initiating them into the worship of the community. Finally, these celebrations may also include the minor exorcisms and blessings mentioned below.

Minor Exorcisms
(RCIA 90-94)

The minor exorcisms are prayers intended to highlight the nature of the Christian vocation, the struggles involved in the spiritual life, and the need for self-discipline, as they invoke God's strength and blessings on the catechumens. Many of these prayers, which may be used more than once (RCIA 93), bear repetition; for example, the prayer in 94B which calls on the power of the Holy Spirit:

we ask you to remove from these your servants
all unbelief and hesitation in faith,
[the worship of false gods and magic,
witchcraft and dealings with the dead],
the love of money and lawless passions,
enmity and quarreling,
and every manner of evil.

And because you have called them
to be holy and sinless in your sight,
create in them a spirit of faith and reverence,
of patience and hope,
of temperance and purity,
and of charity and peace.

The minor exorcisms may be celebrated in conjunction with the celebration of the Word either on Sunday or at catechetical sessions. Not only priests and deacons, but also catechists delegated to do so may celebrate the minor exorcisms and bless the catechumens (RCIA 16, 91, 96–97). In the United States, delegation to perform the rite is assumed in the delegation of the ministry of catechist.

Signs of the provident love of God and the tender care of the Church, blessings accompanied by a laying on of hands are given at the conclusion of celebrations of the Word or of sessions with the catechumens (RCIA 95–97). This ancient practice of invoking a blessing on the catechumens as they continue their journey of faith retains its power to inspire, strengthen, and move them today.

Blessings
(RCIA 95-97)

When sponsors are present, it is desirable to involve them in the blessings and exorcisms. They may simply place their hands upon the shoulder of their candidate as the celebrant prays, or the sponsors may surround the catechumens as the prayer is offered.

In accordance with the decision of the NCCB, the anointing with the oil of catechumens by a priest or deacon is to be done during the catechumenate in order to strengthen the catechumens (RCIA 33, 7). Where desirable for pastoral reasons, the celebration of anointing may be repeated (RCIA 98, 100). The anointing, using oil blessed by the bishop at the

Chrism Mass, is to be administered at the end of the celebration of the Word (RCIA 100–101).

Anticipation of Rites
(RCIA 79, 98, 100-105)

Although the ordinary time for presentations of the Creed and the Lord's Prayer is during Lent, they may be anticipated at a moment during the catechumenate when the catechumens have matured in their faith and commitment (RCIA 98, 104, 148, 157). The rites represent the handing on of the summary of Christian faith (Creed) and the Christian way of praying (Lord's Prayer) (RCIA 147). The celebration may also include the ephphetha rite, or the opening of the ears and mouth. The anticipation of the rites is especially desirable when the catechumenate covers a period of more than a year, so that rather than celebrating all of them during the brief forty days of Lent, these rites can mark progressive points in the catechumens' journey.

The variety and nature of the liturgical rites during the catechumenate indicate that they are integral to the pastoral formation of the catechumens and are not to be omitted. Catechetical sessions that habitually omit prayer with and for the catechumens are manifestly not in accordance with the spirit of the Rite of Christian Initiation of Adults. Moreover, from time to time throughout the year, the whole community should be gathered for some of the rites of the catechumenate (e.g., the presentations) (RCIA 80).

Involvement in
Church Ministries

The fourth element in catechumenal formation is involvement in the apostolic activity of the Church. According to the rite, catechumens are to learn how to work actively with the faithful "to spread the Gospel and build up the Church" (RCIA 75, 4). As candidates progressively experience a change of outlook, they should be led to witness to their new way of life in faith through involvement in ministry. Conversion is evidenced in its social consequences. It is significant in the postconciliar Church that active involvement forms an integral part of the catechumens' ecclesial formation.

ROLE OF
CATECHUMENS

Nourished by the Word of God, sustained by liturgical celebrations, and supported by the community of the faithful, catechumens continue their paschal journey. During the catechumenate period, they strive to respond to God's call by deepening their faith and conversion, by growing in the consciousness of the paschal dimensions of their lives, and by the integration of their faith into their way of life.

Conversion is a complex phenomenon. It is important that those who guide catechumens understand the many modes of conversion and assist catechumens to reflect on where they are in their journey of faith.

Deepening of Faith and Conversion

Conversion involves a transformation of consciousness. For those who have undertaken the path of conversion and faith, there are milestones on the journey. Entrance into the catechumenate assumes several levels of conversion,[1] among them: theistic conversion, that is, faith in God the Creator; and Christian conversion, an acceptance of Jesus Christ as sent by God for the salvation of all people and a desire to follow him as the Way. These modes of conversion lead to an understanding of Church as People of God and a desire for incorporation into the community of believers. This is ecclesial conversion. Other modes include intellectual, attitudinal, and moral conversion, which result in new behaviors.

Transformation involves pain. The journey of faith requires the disciple to leave all in order to follow Christ. The pattern of conversion, as of all Christian life, is to let go, to leave behind all that is not lifegiving and to reach out to new growth, new life in Christ. It is a process of dying and rising. The growing recognition of the paschal mystery as the paradigm of Christian life characterizes the progress of the catechumens' journey. It brings unity and meaning to all the events of life and enables them to hope in the midst of crisis and conflict, which are understood as part of the pattern of life and growth.

Consciousness of the Paschal Dimension of Their Lives

Conversion involves change at the very core of life.[2] The intellectual, attitudinal, and moral dimensions of conversion, referred to above, are manifested in a gradual reordering of

Integration of Faith and Life

---

[1] For a description of the modes of conversion, cf. Edward K. Braxton, "Adult Initiation and Infant Baptism," (section IV) in *Becoming a Catholic Christian*, pp. 174–177.

[2] For a description of dimensions of the conversion process, cf. the citation of Bernard Marthaler in "The Stages of Initiation II. The Catechumenate" by Thomas P. Ivory, *Becoming a Catholic Christian*, p. 106. The section quoted appeared originally in "Catechetical Dimensions of Marriage Encounter," *Origins*, vol. VII, 9 (August 11, 1977): 131.

values, which results in a changed way of living. Christ becomes part of decisions/actions. New dimensions of life are unveiled, as inwardly catechumens discover the mystery of God and of human existence, while outwardly they grow in sensitivity to the implications of this new awareness in both the personal and social dimensions of their lives.

Although not specified in the rite, there is an underlying assumption that those who accompany catechumens on their journey—especially sponsors, catechists, pastors, and those with gifts of spiritual guidance—will assist them in the process of integrating new awarenesses and support them in transitions throughout the period of initiation.

GODPARENTS

During the course of the catechumenate, godparents are chosen (RCIA 80). Catechumens should be encouraged to think about the choice of godparents and discuss it with the pastor or a person designated by him.[3] Often if the sponsor is a member of the local parish, has been involved in the whole process of initiation, and has developed a relationship with the catechumen, he/she becomes the godparent. However, another person may be chosen. In either case, the godparent's role officially begins with Rite of Election. The godparent is to serve as witness and guide. The relationship between candidate and godparent continues beyond the reception of the sacraments of initiation. As stated in the rite, godparents are "to guide the candidates' progress in the baptismal life" (RCIA 11).

Since the ministry involves offering affective personal support to the candidates, godparents should be persons close to the catechumen who have an appreciation of the challenge of the Gospel and desire to share it. Since this is an ecclesial ministry, godparents must be designated for this function by the local community with the approval of the priest (RCIA 11).

CONCLUSION

The catechumenate is the very heart of the process of Christian initiation. The interest and involvement of the community of the faithful provide support and encouragement on

---

[3] For the criteria for the choice of godparents and the liturgical dimensions of their ministry, cf. chapter VII, p. 83.

the way. In this context catechumens grow in faith and commitment until they are ready to enter into a covenant relationship with Christ in the Church through baptism. The witness of their faithful response is a powerful catalyst for renewal in the parish community.

Suggested Reading

(Chapter IV)

The Rite of Christian Initiation of Adults, nos. 9, 2; 16; 41–105; 147–148; 157.

Dujarier. *The Rites of Christian Initiation,* chapters 1–2.

Dunning. *New Wine: New Wineskins,* chapter 3.

Ivory, Thomas P. "The Stage of Initiation: Part II. The Catechumenate." In *Becoming a Catholic Christian,* pp. 104–115. New York: William H. Sadlier, Inc., 1978.

Kemp. "Second Stage: The Catechumenate." *A Journey in Faith.*

Study Guide

(for use with groups)

To develop an appreciation of the breadth of Christian formation during the catechumenate period.

PURPOSE

To explore the role of the parish and the catechumens during this stage.

1. In what ways does the parish community fulfill its supportive role vis-à-vis catechumens? How can parish awareness and support be developed?

QUESTIONS FOR REFLECTION

2. What are the catechumenal ministries in the parish? How are ministers prepared for their roles? What recommendations for development would you make?

3. How does the parish provide for reflection by cate-chumens on the Sunday Liturgy of the Word?

4. Is the dismissal rite after the homily used? Has it ever been tried? If so, what is the effect? If not, why not?

5. What are the elements involved in a catechumenal session in your community? Are there others that should be included?

6. How are the catechesis and the liturgies of the cate-chumenate period integrated into the seasons of the church year? What improvements, if any, would you suggest?

Chapter V
Purification and Enlightenment
(RCIA 118-204)

Step/Doorway	Period	Role of Church	Task of Candidate	Length
Rite of Election or Enrollment of Names	Purification and Enlightenment	Parish Lenten observance; scrutinies, presentations; preparation of candidates for Sacraments of Initiation	Intense spiritual preparation for Sacraments of Initiation	Lenten season (Ash Wednesday–Holy Thursday)

At the beginning of Lent, the Church celebrates the Rite of Election (also known as the Enrollment of Names). The rite celebrates the choice, on the part of the Church, of those to be admitted to Easter baptism[1] (RCIA 118). As in each "doorway" or "step" in the process of initiation, the intention of the Church is to mark the passage to a new level of faith and incorporation into the ecclesial body.[2]

Prior to the celebration, several matters must be decided. The Church, through its delegates, must make a decision regarding the readiness of the catechumens. For their part, the catechumens must decide whether or not they wish to progress to the next period and receive the Easter sacraments. Finally, godparents must be chosen if the choice has not been made previously.

The rite recommends that those involved in the training of the catechumens—catechists, priests, deacons, sponsors, as well as godparents and others delegated by the commu-

---

[1] Baptism is used here in an inclusive sense; that is, water baptism and the sealing with the Spirit in confirmation. Because of the integral nature of these sacraments of initiation, which has been restored by the rite, baptism and confirmation should never be separated in the Christian initiation of adults.

[2] For an informative treatment of the nature of the RCIA, cf. Andre Aubry, "The Pastoral Dimensions of the Rite of Adult Initiation," in *Christian Parish & Rebirth & Renewal* (Washington, D.C.: Federation of Diocesan Liturgical Commissions [FDLC], 1976), pp. 16–30.

nity—meet with the catechumens to deliberate on their readiness for election (RCIA 122). Readiness for this step is indicated by signs of:

- conversion of mind and conduct;
- a sense of Christian faith and charity;
- sufficient acquaintance with Christian teaching;
- a deliberate intention of receiving the sacraments of the Church (RCIA 120).

What the Church is assessing, through gatherings of those who have accompanied the catechumens and through interviews with the catechumens themselves, is the fruits of their conversion. Interior conversion manifests itself in attitudes and behavior. Charity, the greatest of virtues, is the hallmark of Christians. True to its call, the Church expects that conversion of heart will be demonstrated in attitude and in works of charity.

Besides Christian attitudes as manifested in their lives, catechumens must also evidence sufficient awareness of the teachings of the Church. Scripture and the development of its teaching throughout the ages form the rich legacy handed on by the Church to each new generation of believers. A certain assimilation of the knowledge and spirit of this tradition is required prior to baptism. However, it is not simply a question of theological knowledge. Rather, candidates are expected to have entered into an understanding and an experience of the Church's lived tradition. This understanding is evidenced by a new outlook that inspires action and identification with the Christian community, rather than purely objective knowledge. In order to be enrolled, along with this enlightened faith, candidates must have decided that they wish to receive the sacraments of the Church (RCIA 118).

Once the evaluations have been completed, the names of those recommended for election are communicated to the whole parish community and to the bishop for their decision (RCIA 121). It is clear that the involvement of the whole community in the election assumes that the community has been involved in the formation of the catechumens.

The Decision of the Catechumens

At this transition, as in the previous stage, it *cannot be assumed* that every candidate is ready for election. In order to allow the catechumens to make a free choice, it is advisable to allow some time between the end of the catechumenate and the Rite of Election or Enrollment of Names. During this time, interviews between the catechumen and a member of the catechumenal team may be held. These encounters provide the occasion for the candidate to discuss his/her readiness and intention of progressing to the next period. The interviewer should strive to create an atmosphere of trust that will encourage the catechumen to bring up any matter of concern, to ask questions, and/or to seek counsel. As at the previous stage, options should be made clear. The candidate may choose to remain a catechumen until such time as he/she is ready to proceed to the period of immediate preparation for the sacraments of initiation, or the candidate may state the desire, sense of readiness, and intention of pursuing baptism at that time.

"The election, marked with a rite of such solemnity, is the focal point of the Church's concern for the catechumens" (RCIA 121). Having prepared for the celebration of the Rite of Election through assessment of the readiness of candidates (RCIA 122), choice of godparents[3] (RCIA 123), and preparation of the catechumens for the rite, the community proceeds with the liturgical celebration. The Rite of Election or Enrollment of Names is ordinarily celebrated on the First Sunday of Lent (RCIA 128).[4]

Rite of Election

Election, as well as the whole process of conversion, is God's work through the Church. The bishop, as head of the local Church, presides at the election personally or through his delegate (RCIA 125). When a delegate presides, reading from the letter of delegation is recommended to indicate clearly that the election is the activity of the whole Church."[5]

Although the Rite of Election may be celebrated in the parish, increasingly in dioceses where it is practical, ordinaries are inviting the elect to the cathedral for this rite to celebrate the unity of the Church. Many dioceses encourage the sharing

---

[3] Cf. chapter VII of this Study Text for a discussion of the role of sponsors and godparents.

[4] When celebrated on another day, cf. RCIA 128.

[5] For a pastoral explanation of the role of the bishop in the Rite of Election, cf. Raymond Kemp, *A Journey in Faith*, pp. 130–131.

of testimony at a morning celebration in the parish. Later the cathedral celebration of the election takes place within the context of a Service of the Word or an Evening Prayer.

During the rite, it is the bishop's responsibility to set forth the meaning of election and make public the Church's decision regarding those to be enrolled (RCIA 125). Having questioned the representatives of the Church and the candidates, the bishop ratifies the apostolic activity of the parish, which has formed the catechumens, and assumes their decision in the name of the Church.

The rite consists of a presentation and examination of the candidates, the admission or election, followed by prayer for the elect, and a dismissal.

Presentation and Examination of the Candidates

At the conclusion of the Liturgy of the Word, the homily is preached. It focuses on God's call through the Church and on the responsibility of the faithful to witness to the elect by the example of their lives while preparing with them for the Easter solemnities (RCIA 125, 129). The election is then celebrated (RCIA 121). The rite marks a new moment of incorporation for the catechumens. From this time forward, catechumens and faithful journey together. All of the Lenten rites will be celebrated in the context of the community of the faithful.

During the rite, the priest or a person delegated by the community who has been responsible for the formation of the catechumens, presents them to the bishop (RCIA 130). Whenever possible, the celebrant calls each candidate and godparent by name (RCIA 123, 130). The candidates come forward with their godparents. When, due to large numbers, candidates cannot be called forth individually, the rite indicates that this call should be celebrated by catechists and their candidates prior to the common celebration. Where the Rite of Election is held at the cathedral or another central church, the call may be celebrated amid the local community and the candidates sent forth by the parish to the celebration of election.

The celebrant questions the godparents on the suitability of the candidates and hears their testimony. The congregation may then be asked to signify its assent (RCIA 131).

The community of the faithful having indicated its mind, the celebrant then turns to the catechumens. He asks them to state publicly their intention to receive the sacraments of entry into the Church. Once they have done so, the celebrant instructs them to give their names to be enrolled. Candidates may personally inscribe their names in the Book of the Elect or this may be done by the godparent or priest. Godparents may also be asked to sign the register with the candidates (RCIA 123, 132). Where there are large numbers of candidates, a list of names is presented to the celebrant (RCIA 132). Following a brief explanation of the meaning of the rite, the celebrant proclaims the election, exhorts the elect to fidelity, and reminds the godparents of their responsibility toward the candidates (RCIA 133). The whole community then joins in prayer over the elect (RCIA 134).

The celebrant reminds the elect that they have begun the Lenten journey. Before the dismissal, he recalls the upcoming scrutinies (RCIA 136). The elect depart to reflect on the Lenten Word of God and the celebration of their election, while the faithful celebrate the Eucharist.[6]

The catechumens are now known as the "elect" or the "competentes," that is, those who "are joined" together to receive the sacraments of initiation. Other titles designating the elect are those who will be "enlightened" or "illumined" by the light of faith (RCIA 124). These names, reminiscent of the ancient tradition of the Church, have a strange ring in North American culture. The rite encourages the choice of terms better suited to communicate their meaning.

Two elements emerge in the celebration of this rite. First, the dynamic of the rite: the celebrant enters into dialogue with all involved—godparents, candidates, the assembled faithful. Having heard the testimony of all, the celebrant publicly proclaims, not a personal decision, but the decision of the Church. Second, the ordinary celebrant of the Rite of Election or Enrollment of Names is the bishop. In his symbolic role the bishop stands, not only for the entire local Church, but also as the link between all local churches. His presence marks the occasion as a celebration of the Church universal, thus broad-

---

[6] For reflections on the dismissal, cf. chapter IV of this Study Text, p. 47.

ening the horizons of both faithful and elect to the dimensions of the People of God. The presidency of the bishop clearly signifies that incorporation is not simply into the parish, but into the universal Church.

When the candidates are to be sent to the bishop, an optional rite for the Sending of Catechumens for Election is provided so that the parish community may have the opportunity to express its approval of the catechumens and send them forth to the celebration of election assured of the parish's care and support (RCIA 106–117).

PERIOD OF
PURIFICATION AND
ENLIGHTMENT

The period of purification and enlightenment initiated by the Rite of Election normally coincides with Lent (RCIA 126, 138). Lent is the Church's annual retreat, a time of intense spiritual renewal for the entire community. Through prayer, fasting, and good works the People of God deepen the personal and social dimensions of their conversion. For the elect, this is a time of preparation for new life in Christ through baptism. For those preparing for incorporation into the Catholic communion, as for the community of the faithful, it is a time to journey to the sources of their faith and to grow in fidelity to their baptismal commitment in preparation for covenant renewal at Easter.

The RCIA envisions the entire Lenten season in relation to this feast:

In the liturgy and liturgical catechesis of Lent the reminder of baptism already received or the preparation for its reception, as well as the theme of repentance, renew the entire community along with those being prepared to celebrate the paschal mystery, in which each of the elect will share through the sacraments of initiation (RCIA 138).

Now together the entire community—catechumens and faithful—join in preparation for the solemn celebration of the paschal mystery during the Easter Triduum.

The season's central theme is conversion and renewal. Lenten prayer and penance foster the deepening of conversion through the surrender of all that remains of evil or selfishness (purification) and increases openness to God's grace (enlightenment). In it the paschal paradigm of dying and rising is kept clearly in focus, as Christians personally and corporately move forward on their journey to new life and growth in Christ.

In addition to the Sunday celebration of the Liturgy of the Word, the spiritual and catechetical preparation of the elect is completed in the scrutinies, the presentations, and the preparatory rites (RCIA 141, 147, 185).

Since the Lenten season is to be celebrated in the context of the community of the faithful, and since its celebrations are focused on the deepening of conversion and adherence to Christ, they are integral to the preparation of the elect for the celebration of the Easter sacraments.

Liturgy of the Word

When there are candidates for Easter baptism, the readings of Cycle A should be used, in accordance with the norms of the introduction to the lectionary and the indications in the RCIA (RCIA 143, 146).[7]

Each Sunday of this cycle moves the assembled believers forward in their reflection on baptism in Christ and on a way of life rooted in the paschal mystery. In particular, the gospel pericopes open up the riches of the Church's ancient Lenten tradition to contemporary believers. The first Sundays place before us Jesus' forty days of fasting and temptation in the desert (purification) and the glorious moment of his Transfiguration (enlightenment).

On the third to fifth Sundays, the great discourses from John's Gospel, with their remarkable progression of baptismal symbols, are proclaimed:

3rd Sunday	Jn 4:5-42	the Samaritan woman at well	WATER
4th Sunday	Jn 9:1-41	the cure of the man born blind	LIGHT
5th Sunday	Jn 11:1-45	the raising of Lazarus	LIFE

Either a priest or a deacon may preside as the community celebrates the scrutinies following the homily on the third, fourth, and fifth Lenten Sundays (RCIA 145, 146). According

SCRUTINIES

---

[7] Cf. *Lectionary for Mass: Introduction* in *Liturgy Documentary Series 1* (Washington, D.C.: United States Catholic Conference Office of Publishing and Promotion Services, 1982), p. 37.

to the rite, the readings from Cycle A with their proper chants are to be used:

> In every case the ritual Masses "Christian Initiation: The Scrutinies" are celebrated and in this sequence: for the first scrutiny the Mass with the gospel of the Samaritan woman; for the second, the Mass with the gospel of the man born blind; for the third, the Mass with the gospel of Lazarus (RCIA 146).[8]

These readings complete the instruction of the elect on the need for redemption and on the effects of God's saving action. They present Christ the Redeemer as the source of living water, of light, and of life (RCIA 143). The sacramentary contains proper prayers and prefaces based on these Gospels for use in Masses where these scrutinies are celebrated.[9] It is neither good pastoral or liturgical practice, nor is it according to the norms contained in the rite, to use the readings of cycles B or C in liturgies during which the scrutinies are celebrated.

The scrutinies have for their purpose the healing of what is weak or sinful in the hearts of the elect and their strengthening in all that is good and holy (RCIA 141). They are not intended to be an examination of the candidates' worthiness, since no one can be worthy of God's call. What then are the scrutinies? They are celebrations of the honest struggles of the elect in their response to God's call. During the scrutinies, the community prays for the candidates' continued healing and strength. Liturgical planners should note, the texts of the prayers were prepared with candidates for baptism in mind. They should be adapted if used for candidates for full communion into the Catholic Church.

The rite consists of prayer for the elect, in the form of general intercessions; a prayer of exorcism, accompanied by a laying on of hands; and a dismissal. During the Eucharist which follows, a remembrance of the elect and their godparents is included in the eucharistic prayer (RCIA 150–156, 164–177).

---

[8] Cf. *Lectionary for Mass,* nos. 745–747.

[9] Cf. RCIA 150, 164, 171; also in *The Sacramentary* (New York: Catholic Book Publishing Company, 1974), pp. 826–827.

While the faithful are praying over the elect, godparents place their right hands on the shoulder of the candidate they are sponsoring (RCIA 153, 167, 174). It may also be desirable to invite the community of the faithful to extend their right hands, in a gesture of prayer, toward the candidates during the intercessions. By the rite of exorcism, the elect are freed from the effects of sin and strengthened on their journey by the prayer of the Church (RCIA 144). The purpose of the rite is to liberate the candidates from whatever keeps them from fully accepting the Christian life. It is in the midst of a sinful world that they move toward the font. The Church prays that they may be delivered, not only from personal sin, but also from the influence of evil at work in the world. The prayer may be followed by a laying on of hands (RCIA 154, 168, 175).

The profession of faith and general intercessions may be omitted in these Masses (RCIA 156). In this case, petitions for the needs of the whole Church and the world should be added to the prayer for the elect (RCIA 153).

When they have not been anticipated (cf. RCIA 104–105), the presentations are to be celebrated in the weeks following the first and third scrutinies (RCIA 147–149, 157, 178). The presentations are complementary to the scrutinies. As the scrutinies have for their purpose the purification of the elect, so the presentations are intended for their enlightenment (RCIA 141, 147). During these rites, the Church hands over to the elect the summary of its faith in the Creed and the summary of its way of prayer in the Lord's Prayer.[10]

The Presentations

The presentation of the Creed, celebrated during the week following the first scrutiny, ritualizes the traditio, or "handing on" of the faith. It both summarizes and celebrates the activity of the Church during the catechumenate. Before their baptism, candidates will be called to the reditio—the rendering or public proclamation of the Creed—as a profession that the faith of the Church is indeed their faith (RCIA 193, 196). The rite designates special readings for Masses when the Creed is presented (RCIA 158–159). To promote understanding and to avoid the complex theological language of the Nicene Creed,

Presentation of the Creed (RCIA 148, 157–161)

---

[10] Cf. chapter IV of this Study Text, p. 49.

use of the Apostles' Creed is preferred. The rite closes with a prayer over the elect.

Presentation of the Lord's Prayer (RCIA 149, 178–182)

The presentation of the Lord's Prayer is celebrated during the week following the third scrutiny. Following the readings designated for the celebration (RCIA 179) and the presentation, the celebrant explains the meaning of the Lord's Prayer in the homily. The rite closes with the prayer over the elect.

Preparation Rites on Holy Saturday (RCIA 185–186, 193–203)

In the ancient Church, the paschal fast was undertaken from the evening of Holy Thursday through the Easter Vigil, as the faithful celebrated the paschal mystery. In this same spirit, the rite recommends that the elect be instructed to rest from ordinary labor in order to observe Holy Saturday as a day of prayer and fast in immediate preparation for the sacraments (RCIA 185, 1). During the day, some of the preparatory rites: the recitation of the Creed, the Ephphetha rite, and if a new name is to be chosen, the Choosing of a Baptismal Name may be celebrated (RCIA 185, 2). In the Church in the United States it is not customary to choose a new name. These rites may be performed within a gathering of the elect and their sponsors in preparation for the Easter Vigil. Reduction of the preparation to a simple "rehearsal" in preparation for the ceremonies of the Vigil does not seem to be in keeping with the spirit of the day.

Suggested Reading

(Chapter V)

The Rite of Christian Initiation of Adults, nos. 118–204.

Dujarier. *Rites of Christian Initiation,* chapters 3–6, on the rites of this period.

O'Dea, Barbara, DW. *Of Fast and Festival. Celebrating Lent and Easter.* (On the seasonal context.) New York/Ramsey: Paulist Press, 1982.

Parker, James. "The Stages of Initiation III. Purification and Enlightenment." In *Becoming a Catholic Christian,* pp. 116–122.

Study Guide

(for use with groups)

To develop an understanding of the period of purification and enlightenment.

PURPOSE

To explore the initiatory character of Lent.

To foster an appreciation of the Lenten liturgies of Christian initiation.

The group leader instructs participants to reflect on the questions below for five minutes.

QUESTIONS FOR REFLECTIONS

1. Who discerns the readiness of catechumens for election? What criteria are used to discern conversion? How might this process be improved?

2. What does the preparation for the Rite of Election or Enrollment of Names consist of, for each of the following groups:

- catechumens?
- godparents?
- the parish community?

What suggestions would you make regarding the preparation of any of these groups?

3. If the Rite of Election or Enrollment of Names is celebrated at the cathedral or another central church, how does the parish accept and send forth its candidates for election?

4. In the celebration of the scrutinies, how is the purpose of liberation and healing brought out? To what extent do homilies link the Gospels with the celebration of the scrutinies? How might their significance be made more evident?

5. Are the presentations anticipated or celebrated during Lent? Why? What recommendations would you make regarding the timing of these rites and/or the manner in which the celebrations are carried out?

6. What might be the impact of Lent celebrated with a clear paschal focus by catechumens and faithful together on:

    a. the elect as they prepare for baptism?
    b. the members of the parish community?

How might parish Lenten celebrations be planned to focus on the journey toward Easter?

Chapter VI

Sacraments of Initiation and Mystagogy
(RCIA 197–200, 206–251)

Step/ Doorway	Period	Role of Church	Task of Candidate	Length
Celebration of Sacraments of Initiation	Postbaptismal Catechesis or Mystagogy	Postbaptismal catechesis, especially through the Sunday eucharistic celebrations	Deepening Christian experience; full integration into the community of the faithful	Easter season (Easter-Pentecost)

With the conciliar restoration of the liturgical year and the celebration of the sacraments of initiation in the context of the Easter Vigil, the three-day Easter feast has once again been restored to its preeminent position as the apex of the liturgical year. It is the solemn celebration of the paschal mystery, *the* mystery of our faith, which is the *key* to the entire celebration. Although the rite does not specify the participation of the elect in the celebrations of the paschal Triduum prior to the Easter Vigil, it is obvious that their participation with the faithful is desirable.

The Triduum begins with the Mass of the Lord's Supper on Holy Thursday, which plunges the Church into the solemn celebration of the Lord's death and resurrection. In preparation for the Easter celebration, not only the elect, but also the community of the faithful are encouraged to observe the paschal fast on Good Friday and Holy Saturday. Community prayer and fasting highlight the corporate nature of the baptismal covenant, through which Christians become one with Christ in his death and resurrection and one with the whole People of God.

During the course of Holy Saturday, some of the rites preparatory to baptism—the recitation of the Creed, the ephphetha or opening of the ears and mouth, and the choosing of a Christian name—may be celebrated (RCIA 22).

SACRAMENTS OF INITIATION

Preparation

Fasting and Prayer

Preparation Rites

69

The recitation of the Creed (the *reditio*) is celebrated only if the presentation of the Creed (the *traditio* or handing on of the symbol of faith) has been previously celebrated (RCIA 186). Moreover, this rite is not to be confused with the profession of faith immediately prior to baptism.[1]

The ephphetha or opening of the ears and mouth indicates the need for God's grace for two purposes: hearing the word and professing the faith (RCIA 198–199). Pastorally, it seems fitting that this rite, if it is used, be celebrated prior to the recitation of the Creed.[2]

The choosing of a new name is not often celebrated in the United States. It is recommended for use primarily in areas where non-Christian religions flourish (RCIA 200), in which case it is ordinarily celebrated during the Rite of Becoming Catechumens immediately following the signing of the cross.

Easter Vigil   The final stage of Christian initiation is the reception of the sacraments of baptism, confirmation, and Eucharist (RCIA 206). The proper context of the celebration of the sacraments of initiation is the Easter Vigil (RCIA 207). The night watch begins with the invitation to keep vigil as the new fire is blessed, the paschal candle lit, and the Easter proclamation sung. On this holiest of nights, the Church recalls the broad sweep of salvation history: Creation; the Exodus, with its passage through the waters of the Red Sea; and the message of the prophets. Through the Word of God, the faithful and the elect hear their call to be participants in the new creation, the covenanted People of God, as they celebrate the Mother of Feasts.

It is in this context that the baptism of new adult members takes place. So essential is this context, that even when for serious reasons the sacraments are to be celebrated at another time (RCIA 26–27), the celebration must be imbued with the spirit of the Easter feast (RCIA 208), and the blessing of the water, with its rich scriptural allusions, is to be included (RCIA 210).

---

[1] Cf. the preceding chapter of this Study Text for other comments on these rites.

[2] For further reflections and pastoral considerations on the introductory rites, cf. Michel Dujarier. *The Rites of Christian Initiation: Historical and Pastoral Reflections* (New York: William H. Sadlier, 1979).

The celebration of baptism is introduced by the Litany of the Saints (RCIA 218–221). Candidates and their godparents gather at the font visible to the assembled faithful. Through these invocations, the assembly transcends time and space, broadening its horizons to the entire communion of saints. It is fitting that the names of the patron saints of those to be baptized be included in the litany.

The blessing of the water, which follows, expresses the religious symbolism of water. In it the Church rehearses the wonderful works of the Lord through water during the course of salvation history: in Creation, in the waters of the Red Sea, and the Jordan to this very night.

Although the allusions contained in the blessing are in a sense repetitions of the readings, their perspective is different. The focus of the Liturgy of the Word is the vigil of the faithful. (The rite has its origin in an era when the faithful kept vigil, while the elect gathered in a baptistry separate from the church to prepare for baptism.) The focus of the blessing of the baptismal water is the application of the heritage of salvation to the candidates soon to be baptized (RCIA 210). The paschal character of all of the rites should be noted. In the blessing, after recalling the unfolding of the paschal mystery and invoking the power of the Spirit upon the baptismal waters, the celebrant prays that "all who are buried with Christ in the death of baptism rise also with him to newness of life." The blessing has for its purpose the highlighting of new life and new birth into the death and resurrection of the Lord through these waters (RCIA 210).

Before the candidates are baptized, the renunciation of Satan and the profession of faith are celebrated. They form a single rite (RCIA 211). The same paschal mystery, already commemorated in the blessing of the water and soon to be celebrated in baptism, is proclaimed in this rite by the active faith of those to be baptized (RCIA 211). Through the renunciation, the candidates *die* to all that is not of Christ. Through the profession of faith, they personally and publicly assume the faith of the Church as their own, thereby preparing themselves for entering into baptismal *life*. Thus, they express their intention of entering into covenant with Christ (RCIA 211).

In the Jerusalem Church of the fourth century, candidates physically turned from west to east in a symbolic gesture of turning their backs on Satan, his pomps and works, and turning eastward in the direction of the sunrise, symbolic of the Risen Son. The clarity of the action dramatized the seriousness of the intention. Then as now, the place of signal importance in the rite remains the public utterance of the candidates' determination to renounce sin and profess allegiance to Christ. Thus, the process of interior conversion that has taken place throughout the catechumenate is made audible and interpersonal.[3]

Baptism The candidates are then called forth to be immersed in the mystery of Christ's death and resurrection through baptism, the high point of Christian initiation (RCIA 209). Through it the elect are numbered among God's children and complete their incorporation into the People of God (RCIA 212).

Water baptism should be a symbolic activity in the fullest sense of that term. According to the rite, baptism is to be carried out so that there will be a *clear understanding* that what is being celebrated is a sharing of Christ's death and resurrection (RCIA 213). Although both baptism by immersion and by infusion are permitted, the symbolism is more clearly stated by the former. Being plunged into the waters of death and rising up to new life in Christ proclaim unequivocally that the rite is not merely a purification rite (RCIA 213). There are two forms of immersion stated in the rite: of the head only or of the whole body (RCIA 226). The concern for decency and decorum in this paragraph indicates that baptism by immersion of the whole body is indeed a possibility to be considered. Although there are difficulties in its implementation, it is worthy of serious pastoral consideration due to the fullness and the clarity of the sign of dying and rising with Christ which it conveys.[4]

Water baptism is followed by the so-called explanatory rites (RCIA 227). The first is used only on occasions when

---

[3] *Cf. Hugh M. Riley, "Christian Initiation," Studies in Christian Antiquity,* vol. 17 (Washington, D.C.: The Catholic University of America Press, Consortium Press, 1974).

[4] With the renewal of understanding of baptismal symbolism, there has been increased interest in baptism by immersion. For insights into how the question is being approached by some United States parishes, cf. *Chicago Catechumenate,* vol. 4, no. 1 (October 1981): 5–7.

confirmation is not celebrated. Since baptism and confirmation are not ordinarily to be separated in the sacramental initiation of adults, the rite is rarely used (RCIA 228). The second, the bestowal of a white garment symbolizing the dignity of the baptized as part of the New Creation, is optional (RCIA 229). This rite is most appropriate where the donning of a new garment follows baptism by immersion. Finally, the newly baptized are given a candle lit by their godparents from the paschal candle. It is accompanied by a mandate to live their vocation as children of the light (RCIA 230).

The rite states an important principle regarding the confirmation of adults, which is not to be overlooked:

Celebration of the Confirmation of Adults

> In accord with the ancient practice followed in the Roman liturgy, adults are not to be baptized without receiving confirmation immediately afterward, unless some serious reason stands in the way. The conjunction of the two celebrations signifies the unity of the paschal mystery, the close link between the mission of the Son and the outpouring of the Holy Spirit, and the connection between the two sacraments through which the Son and the Holy Spirit come with the Father to those who are baptized (RCIA 215).

The restored rite has joined together what historical accident had separated. The restoration is not simply a liturgical nicety. Rather, it highlights the connection between water baptism and the outpouring of the Holy Spirit that specified Christian baptism in the New Testament.[5] So that this relationship may be maintained, the presbyter who conferred baptism or received the profession of faith of a candidate received into full communion with the Catholic Church confirms the candidates (RCIA 232).

The paschal Eucharist is the culmination of the neophytes' sacramental initiation. Baptized into the death and resurrection of Christ and sealed with the Spirit, the newly baptized are led to the table of the Lord. Exercising their royal priesthood, they take part in the covenant meal of Eucharist (RCIA 217). Thus, their incorporation into the Body of Christ

The Neophytes' First Sharing in the Eucharist

---

[5] Cf. Aidan Kavanagh, *The Shape of Baptism*, chapter 1, "The Tradition," pp. 3–80.

is completed. Having shared the bread of life and the cup of salvation, they are one with the faithful. Together they must be the sacrament of the Lord's continuing presence in the world by their participation in his life and ministry.

PERIOD OF POSTBAPTISMAL CATECHESIS OR MYSTAGOGY

The postbaptismal period ordinarily coincides with the paschal season. The newly baptized or neophytes have been fully incorporated into the Church at the Easter Vigil. What yet remains lacking to their formation? If the catechumenal catechesis has succeeded in laying a firm foundation leading to an Easter celebration in which the paschal mystery was experienced in the language of myth and symbol, then new levels of consciousness, which foster deeper levels of Christian awareness, have been touched in the neophytes. Assisting neophytes to articulate this experience is the role of mystagogical catechesis. For *mystagogia* is the root of the word *mystery*. The mysteries of the faith are to be experienced, celebrated, and reflected on during this period.

The true mystagogue, one who assists new members to unravel the mysteries, is skilled in the language of myth and symbol. The task of the catechist during this final period of initiation is to foster appreciation rather than to present didactic catechesis. It is a time for deepening sacramental awareness, for growing awareness of the paschal mystery in their lives and of the mysterious presence of God in the world.

The rite describes how this is to be done in broad strokes (RCIA 244–245). Together with the community, the newly baptized will grow in the perception of the paschal mystery in their lives through progress in meditation on the Gospel, service, and closer community ties celebrated in Eucharist.

The key to this period is meditation, reflective thinking in the context of the community. Mystery of its nature can never be fully comprehended. Through imagination, association, and meditation, triggered by sound liturgical preaching, the newly baptized come to a deeper understanding of the meaning of God's Word and assimilate it in their lives. Through the experience of the liturgical action of the breaking of the bread, they offer thanks to God for his action in their lives and take on a new sense of faith and celebration. Where the rite of dismissal has been used during the previous stages, there is a newness or a sense of freshness after prolonged absence that allows the neophytes to experience the celebration of Eucharist in a new way. They have a new appreciation of the richness of the symbolic action, through which Christ is present among his people to nourish and sustain them, to bond them into communion as the covenanted People of God. Through postbaptismal catechesis and shared reflection on Word and sacrament in and with the Christian community, they perceive reality in a new way. Life, Church, and Word, are envisioned in light of the paschal mystery.

Throughout the postbaptismal period, the community continues to integrate the neophytes through welcome, friendly interaction, and continued help (RCIA 246). The Easter season is an opportune time for providing occasions of community gatherings outside Eucharist.

Already enriched through the liturgical experience of the sacramental initiation of new members and of the liturgical preaching of the season, access to the experience of neophytes inspires and motivates the faithful in their commitment to Christian living. In a sense, the neophytes by their personal witness become the evangelists, and the cycle of conversion and renewal continues. Witness statements of neophytes or their godparents might also be made in the context of Masses of the Neophytes.

It is important that liturgical presiders, planners, and catechists bear in mind that the chief setting for the neophytes' experience of the sacraments and the community is the Masses of the Neophytes (i.e., the Sunday Masses of the Easter season) (RCIA 247). The rite mandates that throughout Eastertime special places in the congregation should be reserved for the neophytes who, accompanied by their godparents and families, should make every effort to be present at these celebrations (RCIA 248). Highly desirable, this sustained presence is difficult to achieve in a culture where holidays and holy days are prepared for over long periods of time and celebrated within a twenty-four hour period. Pastors, catechists, godparents, and liturgical planners, along with the families and friends of the neophytes, will have to make concerted efforts to assure that this period of unraveling the mysteries of Christian life and commitment are sustained.

Masses of the
Neophytes

The lectionary readings for Cycle A are recommended in Masses for Neophytes, since the readings of this cycle have been planned for their benefit (RCIA 247). Good liturgical preaching is of prime importance. Homilists should take time to get an overview of the seasonal readings in order to discern their unity and progression. The scriptural themes of Eastertime focus on the Good News of the resurrection and on the life of the Church. Acts of the Apostles chronicles the life and growth of the New Testament Church. The Gospels of the season proclaim Christ's resurrection along with key aspects of the Church's faith.

Progression of Easter Gospels (A)	Easter day	Jn 20:1–9	Jesus is Risen! . . the empty tomb
	2nd Sunday of Easter	Jn 20:19–31	The centrality of FAITH: of Thomas' confession of faith
	3rd Sunday of Easter	Jn 24:13–35	Sharing a meal; the disciples of Emmaus recognize Jesus in the BREAKING OF THE BREAD
	4th Sunday of Easter	Jn 10:1–10	Jesus, the GOOD SHEPHERD protects his sheep and guides them to fullness of life
	5th Sunday of Easter	Jn 14:1–12	Jesus is the WAY, the TRUTH, and the LIFE
	6th Sunday of Easter	Jn 14:15–21	Jesus will ask the Father and he will send the SPIRIT
	Ascension	Mt 28:16–20	Jesus RETURNS TO THE FATHER; the mandate for MISSION
	7th Sunday of Easter	Jn 17:1–11	JESUS' GLORIFICATION; prayer for his disciples
	Pentecost	Jn 20:19–23	Gift of the SPIRIT; MISSION of the disciples

Enriched by preaching on these Scriptures and by the eucharistic celebration, the newly baptized and the faithful will learn to savor the meaning of the mysteries of faith in their life together as Church. Moreover, even when Christian initiation is celebrated outside of the usual time, use of the texts of these Masses is recommended (RCIA 247).

During Eastertime the final initiation period draws to a close. Gatherings of the neophytes and their sponsors, along with other members of the community (although perhaps fewer in number), are desirable. The purpose of these gatherings, in keeping with the nature of the postbaptismal period, is reflection by the neophytes on the steps by which the Lord brought them through conversion to sacramental incorporation at the Easter Vigil, reflection on the Scriptures of the season, and orientation of the neophytes to mission and ministry. The meetings are sessions of prayer combined with festivity. During this time, the Church's newest members should be led toward active involvement in the ministries of the community.

Other Gatherings

On or close to Pentecost Sunday, a celebration to close the period of postbaptismal catechesis is recommended (RCIA 249). This celebration marks the end of the initiation period and the beginning of a new stage of life in the Church.

Closing Celebration

Over the course of the year, the bishop makes a pastoral visit to the recently baptized members; if possible, he presides over a eucharistic celebration with them (RCIA 251). Such visits are important so that new members may experience the scope of the local Church through contact with its leader. It is important for bishops, in their pastoral office, to experience the effects of the catechumenal initiation process on the people for which they are ultimately responsible, and it is important for the neophytes to celebrate the Easter mysteries with their bishop. Finally, gatherings on the occasion of the anniversary of baptism are recommended as occasions for thanksgiving, sharing of experience, and renewal of commitment (RICA 250). The actions of the community must not lead to the suspicion that its newest members have been forgotten after the period of initiation. Anniversaries provide occasions for renewed contact and festive celebration.

Suggested Reading
(Chapter VI)

The Rite of Christian Initiation of Adults, nos. 206–243; 244–251.

Dunning. "The Stages of Initiation IV. The Sacraments of Initiation and Afterwards." In *Becoming a Catholic Christian*, pp. 123–131.

Kemp. "The Mystagogical Experience." In *Christian Initiation Resources*, 3:4.

Nocent, Adrian, OSB. "The Easter Season." In *The Liturgical Year*, vol. 3. (On the seasonal context.) Collegeville, Minn: The Liturgical Press, 1977.

"Easter's Fifty Days." In *Liturgy*, 3:1 (Winter 1982). Washington, D.C.: The Liturgical Conference.

Study Guide

(for use with groups)

PURPOSE

To develop an appreciation of postbaptismal catechesis in the context of Eastertime.

To explore the nature of the season and its contribution to the integration and Christian formation of the neophytes.

QUESTIONS FOR REFLECTION

1. The Emmaus Gospel is a paradigm of the journey of faith. Read the account in John 24:13–35. What are the phases of the disciples' journey to faith in the Risen Lord?

2. When and how are newly baptized members encouraged to reflect on their personal-communal journey of faith during the mystagogical period?

3. What are some occasions the parish might provide to allow new members of the Church to share their journey of faith with the community? to share in mission?

4. From your experience, what kind of Church experiences touch life and move the hearts of believers to deeper faith and commitment?

5. Who assists neophytes in determing how they might best use their gifts in ministry? How are they integrated into ministries? How might this process be developed?

Chapter VII

Implementation of the Rite of Christian Initiation of Adults

Christian initiation exists for the Church. The catechumenate represents a moment in the growth of a local Church. It is a period of ecclesial life during which new members gradually and progressively become the Body of Christ. The ministries of the catechumenate assure the growth of the Church through the integral formation of the candidates.

Christian initiation takes place within the Church. Since that is the case, the community of the faithful exercises a formative influence on the development of new members. In addition, various ecclesial ministers—sponsors, godparents, catechists, deacons, priests, and the bishop of the local Church—fulfill specific roles.

A key statement at the very beginning of the rite sets forth a summary of the community's role in the initiation of new members. This statement sets a tone that is carried through the entire document:

> The initiation of catechumens is a gradual process that takes place within the community of the faithful. By joining the catechumens in reflecting on the value of the paschal mystery and by renewing their own conversion, the faithful provide an example that will help the catechumens to obey the Holy Spirit more generously (RCIA 4).

Implementation of the catechumenate[1] calls the community, through its leadership, to recognize its untapped potential and to call forth the Spirit's gifts in its members.

Throughout the process, in response to their apostolic vocation, members of the community are called to demon-

MINISTRIES

Community of the Faithful
(RCIA 4, 9, 75, 244)

---

[1] The term "catechumenate" is used here in a broad sense to refer to the entire process of initiation into the Church.

strate their concern for the initiation of adults. Theirs is the role of reaching out to persons seeking Christ, of spreading the faith,[2] and of assisting candidates during the initiation period (RCIA 9). The Church's mission to "Go, make disciples. . . ." is the ministry of all the baptized. The witness of the faithful, in words and works, is integral to the mission of evangelization. Contemporary Catholic Christians, many of whom are unaccustomed to personal involvement in these roles, must be led, challenged, and prepared to assume them.

The rite specifies the role of the community of the faithful through the various periods of the initiation process. From the beginning, the faithful are to demonstrate a spirit of welcome to inquirers. During the precatechumenate, hospitality is shown by engaging in personal conversation with inquirers, welcoming them into homes, and including them in community gatherings (RCIA 9, 1). This assumes a sense of *identity* and parish spirit sustained by ministries, which continue to build the community, along with a sense of *mission* expressed in ministries of apostolic outreach. In addition, it supposes that opportunities are provided for community members to become acquainted with inquirers (e.g., through meetings with parish groups: the parish council, the staff, bible study or prayer groups, and so forth).

Preparation of testimony, based on knowledge of and contact with candidates, deepens the involvement of individual community members while at the same time serving as a catalyst for the interest and involvement of the entire community.

The community's influence is to permeate the catechumenate period. It is through the community's example and support that catechumens are to grow in prayer, learn to witness to their faith, to live their Christian commitment to the point of self-renunciation, and to work actively with others to build up the Church and spread the Gospel (RCIA 9).

The presence and active participation of the faithful in the transitional rites: The Rite of Acceptance into the Order

---

[2] Evangelization, the process through which the Gospel is preached so that faith may be aroused and grow, is to be carefully distinguished from that style of evangelism popular in some areas.

of Catechumens, the Rite of Election or Enrollment of Names, and the Celebration of the Sacraments of Initiation is normative (RCIA 9, 2, 3, 4). During the Rite of Election, designated members of the community are to give "honest and carefully considered testimony" about the catechumens' progress (RCIA 9, 3). Implementation of this norm, still relatively rare, is to be encouraged. It highlights the responsibility of the whole community for adult initiation.

An authentic and moving facet of the witness of the faithful is the acknowledgment that it is also a community of sinners in need of continuing conversion. Each year during Lent, the members examine their relationship to the Lord who died and rose for them and engage in Lenten prayer, fasting, and works of charity in order to renew themselves in preparation for the celebration of the paschal mystery (RCIA 138). The example of Lenten observance by the faithful is a powerful witness to the elect, as together they are purified by prayer and self-discipline and enlightened by God's Word. The Lenten scrutinies and presentations are celebrated in the midst of the community (RCIA 9, 4). In the weeks prior to these rites, the faithful should receive an orientation on their meaning along with an invitation to participate in their celebration.

During the Easter Vigil, the community renews its baptismal covenant even as it receives its newly baptized members into the Church, which continues the reality of Christ's presence and mission in the world. In the weeks that follow, the faithful participate in the Masses for Neophytes. As they accompany the neophytes in their final period of initiation and complete their integration into the community, the faithful deepen their own appreciation of the meaning of the Lord's death and resurrection and of the life of the Church through the liturgical preaching at these gatherings and by sharing with the neophytes (RCIA 244). The neophytes' incorporation into the community not only represents the Church's growth in numbers, but also is in itself a development of the community experience (RCIA 246).

Any candidate seeking admission to the Church is to have a sponsor. Sponsors form a personal link between the candidate and the Church. The sponsor is someone who knows the candidate and has helped him/her during the initial inquiry.

Sponsors
(RCIA 10)

Sponsors accompany inquirers when they request to become catechumens to witness to their moral character, faith, and intention (RCIA 10). The sponsor may also serve as godparent, should that seem desirable, or the godparent may be another person.

Perons undertaking this ministry should be fully initiated members of the Catholic Church, sufficiently mature for this responsibility, and have the time and willingness to undertake this ministry.[3] Sponsors who have experiences in common with the candidate (e.g., age, interests, marital status) should be selected, so that they will be able to relate to some of the difficulties encountered by the candidates. Those chosen should be persons actively involved in the life of the parish. They should receive adequate preparation for their role.

Sponsorship is a ministry of accompaniment, encouragement, and witness. The sponsor's role involves personal support of the candidate through the stages of initiation. Effective fulfillment of this ministry demands a high level of personal commitment.

Sponsors ordinarily:

- participate in sessions along with their candidates;
- serve as sources of information about the Catholic Church;
- listen to the candidates' reflections, questions, doubts;
- share their own faith experience;
- serve as consultants to those responsibile for the catechumenate regarding the progress of the candidates;
- liturgically, witness to the progress in faith and the intentions of the catechumens during the Rite of Becoming Catechumens.

A frequent question in the choice of sponsors is whether or not a spouse may serve in that capacity. The rite does not address the question. Pastorally, opinion is divided. According to one school of thought, spouses are in a unique position to know, help, and witness to the candidate along the way, on condition that the sponsor-spouse is actively involved in

---

[3] Since sponsorship is an ecclesial ministry similar to that of godparent, the qualifications of a sponsor noted here are adapted from those of godparents in the "General Introduction to the Rite of Christian Initiation," no. 10.

the life of the community. Others favor the choice of sponsors beyond the immediate household, so that candidates will experience a broader sense of Church from the beginning. In either case, candidates' spouses should be encouraged to participate in the catechumenate whenever possible, so that they may share the journey of faith together and strengthen the bonds between them.

The renewed ministry of ecclesial sponsorship is crucial to the successful implementation of the catechumenate. Still evolving in the contemporary Church, the sponsor's role is being enriched continually by the experience of those involved in this ministry.

Godparents are chosen by the candidates on the basis of their example, qualities, and friendship. They should be mature persons, who have themselves received the sacraments of initiation, and active members of the Catholic Church. Having one godparent of either sex meets the canonical requirement.[4] However, the candidate may have an additional godparent. Proposed by the candidates, godparents are delegated by the Christian community and approved by the priest (RCIA 11, 123). **Godparents**

The godparents' ministry begins with the Rite of Election when they give witness, on behalf of the catechumens, before the community (RCIA 131). They accompany the candidates in the scrutinies (RCIA 163, 167, 174), in the celebration of sacramental initiation (RCIA 218ff.), and during the period of postbaptismal catechesis (RCIA 248).

Godparents have a ministry of witness and support. Because the godparent is already linked to the candidate by friendship, he/she is well suited to fulfill the responsibilities of this ministry which include:

- showing the candidate how to practice the Gospel in personal and social life;
- Christian witness;
- support in the growth of baptismal life (RCIA 11).

---

[4] Cf. "General Introduction to the Rite of Christian Initiation," no. 10.

The relationship between godparent and candidate is lasting in character. It endures throughout their mutual lifetime. Persons capable and desirous of such a relationship should be chosen for this ministry.

Catechists
(RCIA 16)

Of singular importance in the Christian formation of the candidates are catechists to whom both the progress of catechumens and the growth of the Church is entrusted. Because of the formative influence of their role, catechists should be persons imbued with Christian spirit, so that they will model and foster it among the candidates.[5]

The ministry of chatechists involves wholistic religious formation of candidates in which the various aspects of Christian life are skillfully interwoven. Their role involves teaching:

- rooted in and filled with the spirit of the Gospel;
- adapted to the rhythm of the liturgical year;
- inclusive of reflection on both the candidates' experience and the teachings presented;
- attentive to the inclusion of prayer experience that inegrates the sign and symbols of the church year;
- suited to the catechumens' needs;
- enriched by local customs (RCIA 16).

In addition, catechists—whether clergy or lay—may be delegated to perform minor exorcisms (RCIA 12) and blessings (RCIA 12). Because of their key role, the rite specifies that they should take an active part in the liturgical rites of the catechumenate.

It goes without saying that catechists must be well prepared for their role. They should be solidly formed in the teachings of Christ and the Church and in an understanding of the church year. More specifically, they are to be given an overview of the catechumenal process and the content of the formation of catechumens. Care must be taken that catechists are formed in a spirituality firmly rooted in the paschal mystery.

In some places catechists, having received a broad-based formation in their ministry, are encouraged to specialize in a

---

[5] For the qualities of catechist, cf. *National Catechetical Directory* [NCD] (Washington, D.C.: USCC Office of Publishing and Promotion Services, 1979), nos. 206–211.

particular segment of catechumenal formation (e.g., Church, morality, prayer). Focusing allows catechists to develop familiarity and comfort with the area for which they are responsible and provides variety for the catechumens. This also allows communities to broaden the basis of catechetical leadership.

The bishop is responsible for the formation of catechists. There is serious need to develop centers where communities can send persons, suited for the ministry of catechist, to be formed for this important role.

The role deacons are to play in the catechumenate is left to the decision of each conference of bishops. Where deacons are to be entrusted with the catechumenate, the rite specifies that they are to be adequate in number to allow for the full implementation of its stages and periods wherever needed (RCIA 15).

Deacons

The priest is responsible for the coordination of the pastoral aspects of the catechumenate and for the coordination of catechumenal ministries. He is to oversee the pastoral care of the catechumens, especially those who are experiencing difficulties. He approves the choice of godparents and guides and supports them in their ministry. With catechists and deacons, he provides for the instruction of catechumens (RCIA 13).

Priests
(RCIA 13–14)

Liturgically, besides the celebration of the sacraments of baptism, confirmation, and Eucharist, priests are responsible for the adaptation of the rites (RCIA 13). "Celebrants should make full and intelligent use of the freedom given to them either in *Christian Initiation*, General Introduction[6] or in the rubrics of the rite itself" (RCIA 35). It is through the cumulative pastoral experience of celebrants that the rites will best be adapted to particular groups and cultures.

The priest who baptizes an adult or a child of catechetical age should normally administer confirmation within the same liturgical event. Where numbers are large, other priests having particular offices or functions in the diocese or having a par-

---

[6] NCD, no. 34.

ticular relationship to the candidates may assist in administering the sacrament (RCIA 14).

Priests should know the candidates and their godparents. In no case should priests confine their personal ministry to catechumens to presidency at liturgical rites.

BISHOP   The bishop is the leader of the liturgical life of the church committed to him.[7] In relation to the catechumenate, the responsibilities of the bishop fall into two main categories: those for which he is to make provisions and those he exercises personally or through a delegate. His role is

- to set up, regulate, and promote the pastoral formation of catechumens;
- to admit candidates to their election and to the sacraments;
- to preside at the Lenten liturgy;
- to appoint catechists to celebrate minor exorcism;
- to celebrate personally the Rite of Election or to ratify the admission of the elect personally or through a delegate;
- to celebrate personally the Easter Vigil and the sacraments of initiation;
- to meet with new members at least once a year;
- to determine whether and when the Rite of Initiation may be celebrated outside the ordinary times;
- to dispense from one or two of the scrutinies (RCIA 34, 251).

What the rite highlights is the role of the bishop as "overseer" and head of the local Church, responsible for its life and growth. In that capacity, he is to pay particular attention to the quality of formation given to new members. It is through pastors and the pastoral offices of the diocese, primarily those of worship and catechesis, that the bishop works for the implementation of the catechumenate.

By assuming active leadership in the catechumenate, the bishop sees to its integration into the rhythm of church life. It is his task to assure that there are active catechumenates throughout the diocese to provide for the needs of those who

---

[7] NCD, no. 12.

wish to enter the Church. To assist pastors in setting up catechumenates and to assure the quality of catechesis, the bishop can provide services that facilitate the implementation of the rite (e.g., setting up diocesan or regional centers for the formation of catechists). The bishop's participation in the Lenten rites witnesses to his personal interest, not only in the catechumens, but in the growth of the Church. In particular, it is his prerogative to preside at the Rite of Election when, acting in the name of Christ and of the Church, he admits the elect (RCIA 125). When the bishop cannot personally preside at the election, he designates a delegate. Where catechumens are numerous or the diocese geographically spread out, the rite may be held in several centers in the week preceding or following the first Sunday of Lent (RCIA 126).

The bishop presides at the Easter Vigil, ordinarily at the cathedral church, and administers the sacraments of initiation.

Through the pastoral office of the bishop, candidates experience the bonds that unite the parish community to the local and universal Church. During the course of the initiation period or at least once in the year that follows, the bishop meets with them (RCIA 251).

Involvement of the bishop in the catechumenal process shapes the local Church, catechumens, and faithful. Once again the centrality of baptism-confirmation and Eucharist is restored.

Two pivotal points are clearly enunciated in the norms for the right of initiation: 1) the sacraments are celebrated at the Easter Vigil; 2) the election takes place on the First Sunday of Lent (RCIA 17). Although it is lawful in extraordinary circumstances to schedule the rite differently, this is to be done only with permission of the bishop (RCIA 17, 26, 34). Even in these cases, the catechumenal process and the celebration of the rites must be imbued with the paschal character and spirit.

TIME AND PLACE OF INITIATION (RCIA 18–31)

In the introductory paragraph to this section (RCIA 18), the rite contains important cautions. First of all, to begin the precatechumenate, a number of prospective inquirers should be gathered. Parishes have begun successfully with as few as

Proper or Usual Times

two inquirers. Clearly, individual convert instruction is no longer the way to incorporate members into the Church. Inquirers should be able to begin some association with a parish when they present themselves. Introduction to members of the community, inclusion in parish events, and interviews with those responsible for the formation of new members mark the welcome and hospitality of the community and begin the process of inclusion.

Second, entrance into the order of catechumens should not take place too early. Those responsible for the catechumenate should avoid the tendency to rush the period of inquiry for reasons of efficiency and/or convenience. Particular care in this matter is to be observed where the programmatic aspects of the catechumenate are scheduled to coincide with the school year. Initial faith and conversion are not to be assumed. Rather, two or more dates for the reception of catechumens may be set during the year to respect the rhythm of the inquirers' progress.

The fixed points in the liturgical calendar include:

Rite of Election: First Sunday of Lent (RCIA 19). The rite may be anticipated or delayed somewhat, especially to allow for the presence of the bishop.

Scrutinies: Third, Fourth, and Fifth Sundays of Lent (RCIA 20). For pastoral reasons these rites may be transferred to other Sundays or even weekdays. However, the permission of the bishop is required to omit one or two of the scrutinies where there are serious reasons for so doing. If the election is anticipated, the first scrutiny should also be moved forward. Even in this event, the period of purification and enlightenment should not exceed eight weeks.

Presentations: Weeks following the first and third scrutinies (RCIA 21). The presentations may be anticipated as rites of passage during the catechumenate, especially when it covers a prolonged period of time (RCIA 104–105).

Preparation Rites: Holy Saturday (RCIA 22). If the day is observed in recollection, fasting, and abstinence from work, in the spirit of the rite, the preparatory rites may be celebrated during the course of Holy Saturday.

Sacraments of Initiation: Easter Vigil (RCIA 23). In mission churches where the Easter Vigil is not celebrated, the sacraments may be celebrated within the Easter octave. The Mass of the day or the ritual Mass for Christian Initiation may be used with the readings of the Easter Vigil.

Masses for Neophytes: Sundays of Easter (RCIA 25). Somewhat neglected, these celebrations are important to the sense of inclusion of neophytes. New members, accustomed to intense involvement and to the concern of the Church throughout the catechumenate, are likely to experience a sense of abandonment where no further gatherings are provided. Sustained inclusion and reflection promote commitment and an enduring memory of their first paschal experience.

Although allowed for in the rite, there are sufficient restrictions on the celebrations of the rites outside customary times to underscore the extraordinary nature of this practice. Even when in "unusual circumstances," with the permission of the bishop, the Lenten rites and the sacraments of initiation are celebrated at another time, the Lenten program of initiation, the structure of the entire rite, and the spaced intervals remain the same (RCIA 26).

Outside the Usual Times (RCIA 26–31)

In addition, the sacraments of initiation are to be celebrated on Sunday, in keeping with its character as the day of resurrection (RCIA 27). The Rite of Election is not to be celebrated on a solemnity of the church year, so that the readings in the ritual may be used. In the six-week interval between these two stages, the scrutinies and presentations are to be celebrated (RCIA 29–30).

The primary responsibility for adaptation of the rite itself has been entrusted to conferences of bishops which are to adapt it to the conditions of their respective regions (RCIA 32–33). They provide for the preparation of translations, additions of formulas to the rite (where appropriate), and the preparation of musical settings for the texts. In order to promote the understanding and effective celebration of the rite, they may add introductory material. Their decision on cultural and other adaptations of the rite must be submitted to the Holy See. They have discretionary power to formalize the

ADAPTATIONS

method of receiving inquirers, to insert what would be culturally effective, and to avoid what may be culturally offensive.[8]

The specific decisions of the NCCB are noted in the RCIA 33, 2–33, 8 and have been incorporated into the text in the proper places.

The principal adaptations of the rite, which fall under the authority of the bishop, have been outlined above. In exceptional circumstances, he may also permit use of the simple rite in whole or in part (RCIA 34, 31).

Adaptations by the minister, in the celebration of the rites, are to be carried out with sensitivity to the pastoral context. To encourage pastoral adaptation, the manner of acting and praying, the use of various options, accommodations of the rite to fit the circumstances and needs of the candidates and the assembly are left to the pastoral judgment of the presider (RCIA 35).[9] Such adaptation requires advance planning and careful preparation, so that the rites may be celebrated in a prayerful manner.

Suggested Reading

(Chapter VII)

Holash, Lise M. *Evangelization, the Catechumenate and Its Ministries*, chapters 3–5 on the ministries of catechist, sponsor, and priests, Dubuque: Wm. C. Brown Publishers, 1983.

Lewinski, Ronald. *Guide for Sponsors*. Chicago: Liturgy Training Publications, 1980.

————. *Welcoming the New Catholic*. Chicago: Liturgy Training Publications, 1978.

Villaca, Theophile and Michel Dujarier. "The Various Ministries in Christian Initiation." In *Becoming a Catholic Christian*, pp. 132–143, on the evolution of catechumenal ministries and current pastoral perspectives.

---

[8] NCD, nos. 30–33; cf. also RCIA 33.

[9] NCD, nos. 34–35.

Cf. also "booklets for sponsors." Cincinnati: Archdiocesan Office of Worship and Lakewood, Colo.: Worship Resources, Inc.

Study Guide

(for use with groups)

To explore the ministries and time lines involved in the implementation of the catechumenate.

PURPOSE

1. In the preparation of ministers for the catechumenate in your parish or community

QUESTIONS FOR REFLECTION

   a. What opportunities for training can best be offered on the parish or community level?
   b. What services might the parish request of the diocese?

2. What was the understanding of the sponsor's ministry when the parish began to implement the RCIA? How has this ministry developed through the experience of the catechumenate?

3. How are godparents who have not participated in the catechumenate prior to the election introduced to their ministry?

4. In what areas has the catechumenate team grown and developed? What are the stagnant areas? What recommendations would you make?

5. Beginning with the fixed points of the Lenten and Easter seasons, prepare a schedule for the parish catechumenate, in line with the norms stated above.

Chapter VIII

Pastoral Observations and Directions

The implications of the RCIA, in the areas of spirituality, ministry, and sacramental and pastoral practice, are far reaching indeed. The conclusion of this Study Text on the RCIA will be limited to the exploration of specific areas: the theological unity of the sacraments of initiation and the types of catechumens and candidates. In addition, some implications of the rite, in the areas of pastoral and sacramental practice, will be treated.

The "General Introduction to Christian Initiation" contains a unified theological orientation to the rites that follow: the Rite of Christian Initiation of Adults, Rite of Baptism for Children and the Rite of Confirmation. A common orientation on key theological points is clearly set forth.

THEOLOGICAL AND PASTORAL UNITY OF THE RITES OF CHRISTIAN INITIATION

First of all, the sacramental encounter with God is understood in terms of relationship to the Trinity; death and resurrection with Christ; God's sons and daughters through the Spirit of adoption.[1] Second, baptism, confirmation and Eucharist are clearly set forth as the complete sequence of Christian initiation. Christians are brought to full stature in Christ and enabled to carry out the mission of God's People in the world.[2] Moreover, the close links among the three sacraments are explicitly stated in the proper introduction to each of the rites.[3]

The common aim of the rites is a lively, informed, active, mature faith; therefore, the importance of pastoral instruction of candidates or, in the case of young children, of parents is highlighted. Moreover, faith is understood as a developing reality. In the case of adults, as faith matures, candidates move from one stage of Christian initiation to the next. Infants are baptized into the faith of the community. Parents and godpar-

---

[1] "General Introduction to the Rite of Christian Initiation," no. 1.

[2] "General Introduction to the Rite of Christian Initiation," no. 2.

[3] Cf. RCIA 206, 215; Rite of Baptism for Children, no. 5, (5); Apostolic Constitution on the Sacrament of Confirmation, Pope Paul VI, pp. 1, 3; Rite of Confirmation, no. 1.

ents commit themselves before the Church to nurture and develop the child's faith life.

Further, Christian initiation is understood as an ecclesial event. As such, all three rites present initiation as the concern and the responsibility of God's people. The involvement of the Church through the ministries of catechists, priests, deacons, sponsors, godparents, and others in the preparation of candidates, and the active participation of the assembled faithful in sacramental celebrations of initiation are common to all of the rites.

Although this unified approach is discernable in the overall orientation to the sacraments of initiation, several striking contrasts exist between the process for adults and that for children. These differences lie notably in the areas of the sacramental sequence and the normative times for their celebration.

Sequence
In the Rite of Christian Initiation of Adults, the process is built on a developmental model. The candidate moves from *conversion*—through *catechesis*—to *sacramental initiation*. In the case of infant baptism, the process is reversed. First there is *baptism*—then *catechesis*—to foster *conversion*. The first stresses personal, active involvement on the part of initiates leading to mature faith and commitment. The second emphasizes incorporation into the faith of the Church. The rite implies that there must be reasonable hope that infants will be formed in the faith into which they have been baptized and gradually assimilate it to the point of personal conversion and faith.

Time of Celebration
Ordinarily in the sacramental initiation of adults, baptism, confirmation, and Eucharist are to be celebrated in a unified liturgical event during the Easter Vigil. The ancient order of baptism into the death and resurrection of Christ, sealing with the Spirit, followed by admission to the table of the Lord is respected. The rite insists that confirmation should not be separated from the celebration of baptism, except for serious reasons.

With children, on the contrary, the separation of baptism, confirmation, and Eucharist has been maintained. No reasons

94 ———

are given for this position. Moreover, in an anomalous statement in the introduction to the Rite of Confirmation[4] the traditional order of confirmation, followed by Eucharist, is maintained, although it is clear elsewhere that the preference is for First Communion to take place at the Confirmation Mass.[5] In terms of the season of the celebration of the baptism of children, based on the Johannine mandate (Jn 3:5), the norms continue to associate baptism more closely with the birth of the child than with the paschal feast.[6]

The Church's decision to maintain infant baptism, based on the early tradition of the Church, along with the baptism of adults is clear. The latter underscores the faith response of the adult to God's call; the first highlights God's initiative and the ecclesial nature of the response; both are significant facets of the relationship of God with his people throughout salvation history. In current pastoral practice, the two coexist in tension and complementarity.

Pastoral experience, accompanied by theological reflection, will lead to a clearer understanding of the Church's baptismal policy and perhaps to further revision of the rites.

CATECHUMENS

Faith comes through the grace of conversion. The catechumenate is a catechetical-liturgical structure that has for its purpose the nurturance and development of faith to the point of readiness for sacramental incorporation into the Church through baptism, confirmation, and Eucharist. Strictly speaking, a catechumen is one who has never been baptized and who, in a faith response to the Word of God, asks to be prepared for sacramental initiation in the Church. It is primarily for these candidates that the RCIA is intended.

OTHER CANDIDATES

In the United States however, there are other types of candidates who present themselves to the Church: those partially initiated. These people fall into several categories. They may have been:

- validly baptized Catholics with no subsequent experience of Church;

---

[4] Rite of Confirmation, no. 3.
[5] Rite of Confirmation, no. 13.
[6] Rite of Baptism for Children, no. 8, (3), (4).

- validly baptized Catholics but never confirmed nor communicated;
- baptized and perhaps confirmed in another Christian church, having lived their faith and seeking reception into the Roman Catholic communion.

Pastoral ministers must deal with each inquirer personally in order to determine whether and to what degree the partially initiated should be included in the rites and process of the RCIA. Those baptized but unchurched may, in many ways, have needs similar to those who are catechumens strictly speaking. However, their baptism must be taken into account, and it must not be repeated (RCIA 16). Regarding those fully initiated sacramentally into another communion who have requested reception into the Roman Catholic Church, those candidates may or may not be in need of intellectual, moral, or other levels of conversion. They may need to mature in faith or may simply be candidates for some instruction in doctrine, exposure to Catholic tradition and expressions of piety, and inclusion in the local Church.[7] Discernment of the life and faith situation of each prospective candidate is critical in determining the kind of pastoral experience he/she may require.

While baptized persons who have never been confirmed or received communion will need to be prepared for the reception of these sacraments, they may have other needs. Pastoral ministers should meet with these candidates to determine with them what progress they have made on their faith journey and what needs they may have in the areas of evangelization, conversion, instruction, prayer, and familiarity with the Catholic tradition. It should also be noted that some of this last group may have been baptized in the Catholic Church and brought up in Catholic surroundings. Where this is the case, the needs and questions of the candidate may be sufficiently different from those of other candidates to warrant a different approach to sacramental preparation.

In order that candidates from any of these categories may be incorporated into an adapted form of the catechumenal process, the ritual provides a series of rites for use with can-

---

[7] Cf. Chapter III of this Study Text, p. 33.

didates who have already received the sacrament of baptism. These rites may be used for such candidates alone, or in combination with the rites for the unbaptized.[8] During these rites, however, a clear distinction is made between the two groups of unbaptized and baptized.

Above all, the character and purpose of the catechumenate—the nurturing of conversion and faith from its initial stages through maturity sufficient for the reception of the sacraments of initiation—must be respected. This clearly implies that the catechumenate is *not* a renewal structure, much less an update program for adult Catholics. Renewal of church members, while always of prime pastoral concern to the Church, should be tended to through other opportunities such as, prayer, study, or renewal groups; opportunities for retreats and the observance of the Church's annual seasons of covenant renewal; and celebration during Lent and Easter.

The context for the renewed praxis of Christian initiation is a renewed Church. It is the Church that initiates new members, shaping their Christian identity and their practical expression of faith. Since this is the case, the successful implementation of the revised rite of Christian initiation will be dependent on and proportionate to the successful renewal of the ecclesial context in which it takes place. The mandate to "make disciples" requires of the Church a consciousness of its corporate call to be Christ's presence and to continue his mission in the world.

CONTEXT FOR REVISED RITES

On the spiritual level this implies that Catholic Christians must come to an understanding of the paschal mystery, not simply as a theological concept, but as a continuing reality in the Church. In other words, the whole Church, individually, as well as personally, must experience a renewed sense of its calling to live that mystery in order to be salt, leaven, and light in the world.

Role of Evangelization

The task of adult evangelization and catechesis, within Catholic parishes, is a major challenge. The statement of Pope Paul II in *Evangelii Nuntiandi* is relevant here: "The Church

---

[8] Cf. RCIA, Part II: Rites for Particular Circumstances and Appendix I: Additional (Combined) Rites.

is not only evangelizer, but it begins by being evangelized itself." Through evangelization each generation learns the truth of God's love for the human race in creation and in redemption. Through it believers also experience the truth about human beings: their dignity as created and beloved of God, their sinfulness and separation from God's ways. The aim of evangelization is conversion to the Kingdom of God, that is, to the values of the renewed world inaugurated by the Gospel and to a way of living in the world that contributes to the growth of the Kingdom here and now.

Renewed pastoral theology must focus on conversion and faith as the very genesis of Church.

IMPLICATIONS OF THE RCIA IN AREAS OF SACRAMENTAL AND PASTORAL PRACTICE

One of the far-reaching implications of the RCIA in pastoral practice is that it calls for a true revolution in our approach to Church and sacramental ministry. As stated above, what the rite implies is that the starting point in our definition of Church, as in any description of Christian spirituality, is always conversion and faith.

In the rite, the Church has rediscovered in its tradition a process for fostering the growth of the faith, which identifies it as Christian. The movement is always from the experience of faith to sacramental celebration and never the reverse. That truth is, at times, difficult for the contemporary Church to grasp. However, once understood, it affects all sacramental preparation programs.

SACRAMENTAL PREPARATION

If the RCIA can be a model of sacramental preparation, and if the movement is from experience of faith to sacramental celebration, what steps can be discerned in the process? There are several discernable periods:

1. *Initial period.* The purpose of this period is to get in touch with the human experience that has led persons to seek the sacrament and to deepen motivation to the point where subjects consciously decide to seek the sacramental encounter with the Lord.
2. *Catechesis.* During this period, candidates are led to reflect on their experience in the light of Scripture and tradition. Catechesis may take the form of programs of preparation for reconcilation and baptismal renewal.

It provides Lenten preparation for reconciliation and baptismal renewal. It provides the occasion to reflect on God's call in light of the Scriptures and similar encounters of the holy men and women throughout Christian tradition.

3. *Retreat*. The retreat experience provides the opportunity for deepening the subject's desire and decision to receive the sacrament.

4. *Sacrament*. The sacramental celebration is the apex of the process. Open to God's grace and ready and willing to receive it, recipients appropriate and celebrate God's loving action in their lives.

Thus, sacraments become the culmination of an experience and not the first step.

In this light, the sacrament of penance marks the completion of a process of responding to God's call to reconversion and reconciliation; the anointing of the sick celebrates the candidates' desire and the prayer of the Church for God's gift of inner, as well as physical, wholeness and healing; marriage is celebrated as God's gift of love, which bonds people together in a covenant relationship, which in turn signs God's loving fidelity for his people.

Thus, as in the RCIA, sacraments are experienced as occasions for receiving and celebrating God's love. They celebrate God's gifts to his people and are true symbolic actions that effect what they signify, thereby enabling people to receive gifts of life, love, and reconciliation.

RESTORATION OF THE CATECHETICAL—LITURGICAL RELATIONSHIP

Reflection on the history of the catechumenate reveals the dissolution of the bonds between catechetics and liturgy that took place over the centuries. Initial attempts at restoration of the catechumenate in mission lands ignored this relationship—to their detriment. Sacramentals and pious practices, laudable as they might be, were incapable of bearing the symbolic weight of the passages required by the initiation process. It was only in 1962, in the Church in France, that the catechetical-liturgical integrity of the process was restored, allowing for the full and rich celebration of the periods and transitions of the process. Still today, the interrelation of the two has not been fully restored. Integration of the RCIA into the rhythm of Church life means that serious attention be given to the restoration of the close relationship between these two ministries on every level of Church life. This implies that seminaries must integrate the catechetical dimension into their programs of instruction on sacraments and liturgy. It also demands that colleges and universities integrate courses into the church year and revise current approaches to sacramental catechesis in programs for the preparation of ministers of religious education. In addition, publishers of catechetical materials should be sensitized to the integrity of the liturgical component of all aspects of Christian formation, whether of adults or of children.

On the local level, parish leaders must become conscious of the complementarity of catechetics and liturgy, not only in the implementation of the RCIA, but in the planning of all catechetical, sacramental, and renewal efforts in the parish. The Lent-Easter seasons must become the pivotal points of parish planning. The annual celebration of covenant renewal can spark the ministry and mission of the local Church throughout the year, creating a common commitment that becomes a source of the revitalization of parish life. Finally, ministers of religious education should be sensitive to the incorporation of the liturgical dimension and to the adaptation of curricula to the church year in the choice of materials for use in the catechetical programs in the parish.

In this matter, diocesan offices of worship and offices of religious education must work together to be of assistance to parishes in the evaluation of materials and in the recommendation of programs that support the accomplishment of these goals.

MINISTRIES

Another aspect of church life, in which the Second Vatican Council and the Rite of Christian Initiation call for a turnabout in approach, is the area of ministry. One of the major insights brought forth in this area is that ministry is the responsibility of all baptized Christians. Further, the scope of ministry called for in the implementation of Christian initiation and in the renewal of sacramental preparation alone demands the calling forth of the gifts of many of the faithful and their careful preparation for ministerial roles. In addition, the growing consciousness of the Church's mission in society makes additional demands on local churches for the development of outreach ministries, such as evangelization and social action. What is clear is that ministry in the Church can no longer be restricted to ordained, religious, and professionally trained personnel. Rather, the leaders must become catalysts, in their particular areas of ministry, to activate the Spirit's gifts in the faithful and to form them for ministries in the local Church.

Services of diocesan offices should be directed to offering resources for the training of parish ministers in local areas. In this work, dioceses can coordinate the sharing of personnel and other resources for the training of ministers for parishes.

In the decade following the promulgation of the Rite of Christian Initiation of Adults, the task of pastoral leaders involved assimilation of the rite's contents and meaning and its initial implementation. The challenge of the decades ahead is that of contextualization and acculturation. Contextualization, as used here, means recognizing the catechumens not as yet another parish group, but as an *order* of people integral to the life of the local Church. Acculturation, on the other hand, will result from the response of pastoral ministers on all levels to the mandate of adaptation repeated throughout the rite. Through the careful adaptation of the rites to local cultures, the Church while remaining one, holy, and catholic will become a communion of truly indigenous churches united by a common faith and a common mission in the world.

Suggested Reading

(Chapter VIII)

RCIA, Part II: Rite for Particular Circumstances and Appendix I: Additional (Combined) Rites.

Braxton, Edward K. "Adult Initiation and Infant Baptism." In *Becoming a Catholic Christian,* pp. 162–177.

Guzie, Tad. "Theological Challenges." In *Becoming A Catholic Christian,* pp. 153–161.

Kavanagh, Aidan. *The Shape of Baptism,* chapter 6, pp. 152–203.

Study Guide

(for use with groups)

PURPOSE

To reflect on the implications of RCIA or other dimensions of parish life.

To explore options for responding to the challenge to parish renewal.

QUESTIONS FOR REFLECTION

1. In the case of Catholics baptized as infants, how can subsequent catechesis be geared to foster the experience of conversion and mature faith?

2. How is the parish fulfilling its responsibility to continue the evangelization of members? To what extent is evangelization geared to conversion to the values of the Kingdom of God?

3. Currently, the baptism of infants is more closely associated with the date of birth than with the celebration of the death and resurrection of Christ into which they are baptized. What might be the advantages to the Christian community of celebrating infant baptism in connection with feasts and seasons more closely linked with the paschal mystery (e.g., the Sundays of the Easter season)?

4. How might the liturgical dimension be better integrated into the catechetical, sacramental, and renewal programs of the parish?

Select Bibliography

Bibliographies

Federation of Diocesan Liturgical Commissions (FDLC). "Rite of Christian Initiation of Adults, An Annotated Bibliography." Washington, D.C.: FDLC, 1983. 49 pp.

Gusmer, Charles W. "A Select Annotated Bibliography of the Rite of Christian Initiation of Adults (RCIA)." In *Parish Ministry* 3:6 (March–April 1982): 12–13. An annotated listing of 38 items.

Lewinski, Ronald. "Catechumenate Resources." In *Liturgy 80* (August–September 1981): 17. An annotated listing of 21 books.

Ling, Richard. *Bibliography Resources*. Lakewood, Colo.: Worship Resources, Inc., 1979.

Periodicals

Chicago Catechumenate. Chicago: Liturgy Training Publications. Published five times a year.

Christian Initiation Resources (CIR), James B. Dunning and William J. Reedy, editors. New York: William H. Sadlier, Inc. Published quarterly.

General

[On the Rite of Christian Initiation of Adults]

Ritual editions: USCC Office of Publishing and Promotions; Catholic Book Publishing; Liturgical Press; Liturgy Training Publications.

Study editions: USCC Office of Publishing and Promotions; Catholic Book Publishing; Liturgical Press; Liturgy Training Publications; Pueblo Publishing Company.

DOCUMENTS

BOOKS/COLLECTIONS   Dunning, James B. *New Wine: New Wineskins. Exploring the RCIA*. New York: William H. Sadlier, Inc., 1981.

Federation of Diocesan Liturgical Commissions. *Christian Parish & Rebirth & Renewal*. A collection of papers containing background to the RCIA. Indianapolis: FDLC, 1976.

Hovda, Robert, ed. *Made, Not Born: New Perspectives on Christian Initiation and the Catechumenate*. The history and meaning of the RCIA. Notre Dame: University of Notre Dame Press, 1976.

Kavanagh, Aidan. *The Shape of Baptism: The Rite of Christian Initiation. Studies in the Reformed Rites of the Catholic Church*. vol. 1. New York: Pueblo Publishing Company, 1978.

Kemp, Raymond B. *A Journey in Faith: An Experience of the Catechumenate*. New York: William H. Sadlier, Inc., 1979.

O'Dea, Barbara, DW. *The Once and Future Church*. Kansas City, Mo.: Celebration Books, 1980.

Reedy, William J., ed. *Becoming a Catholic Christian: A Symposium on Christian Initiation*. New York: William H. Sadlier, Inc., 1978. 198 pp. (Reviewed by Thomas E. Kramer in *Worship* 53:2 [March 1979]: 165–167.)

_____ . "Christian Initiation into Full Community." In *National Bulletin on Liturgy* 11:64 (May–June 1978).

ARTICLES   Aubry, Andre. "The Pastoral Dimensions of the Rite of Adult Initiation." In *Christian Parish & Rebirth & Renewal*, pp. 16–30. Indianapolis: FDLC, 1976.

Beraudy, Roger. "The New Ritual for Adult Baptism." In *Theology Digest* 24:1 (Spring 1976): 57–62.

Cunningham, Joseph L. "The New Ritual of Adult Initiation." In *Simple Gifts*, edited by Gabe Huck, vol. II Washington, D.C.: The Liturgical Conference, 1974; also in *Worship Resources Newsletter* 2:9 (February 1974).

Duffy, Regis A. "My Fellow Beginners." In *Christian Initiation Resources,* edited by James B. Dunning and William J. Reedy, 2:1 (1981). 6 pp.

Duggan, Robert. "Implementing the Rite of Christian Initiation of Adults: Pastoral-Theological Reflections." In *The Living Light* 17:4 (Winter 1980): 327–333.

Gusmer, Charles W. "How Do Liturgists View Initiation?" In *Christian Initiation Resources,* edited by Dunning and Reedy, 1: 1 (1980):14–19.

_____ . "Who Are the Catechumens?" In *The Chicago Catechumenate* 4:5 (July 1982): 5–12.

Hanson, Donald M. "The Rite of Christian Initiation: An Introduction." In *Christian Initiation Resources,* edited by Dunning and Reedy, 1:1 (1980) 7–13.

Kavanagh, Aidan. "Adult Initiation: Process and Ritual." In *Liturgy* 22:1 (January 1977): 5–10.

_____ . "Initiation." In *Liturgy* 18:7 (August–September 1973): 4–8. Reprinted in *Simple Gifts,* edited by Gabe Huck, vol. II. Washington, D.C.: The Liturgical Conference, 1974.

_____ . "The Norms of Baptism: The Rite of Christian Initiation of Adults." In *Worship* 48:3 (March 1974): 143–152. Reprinted by Worship Resources, Inc. Reprinted, in part, in *Christian Parish & Rebirth & Renewal,* pp. 31–36. Indianapolis: FDLC, 1976.

_____ . "Unfinished and Unbegun Revisited: The Rite of Christian Initiation of Adults." In *Worship* 53:4 (July 1979): 327–340.

Ling, Richard. "The Catechumenate: A Symbolic Giant." In *Worship Resources Newsletter* 5:10–11 (July 1980). Also available under the title *What Is the Catechumenate?* cassette A747. Kansas City, Mo.: NCR Cassettes.

Mick, Lawrence E. "Catechumenate for Adults." In *New Catholic Encyclopedia,* vol. XVII, pp. 79–80.

_____ . "Looking to the Future." In *Today's Parish* 8:8 (November–December 1976): 42–43.

Reedy, William J. "A Forum on Ecclesial Conversion." In *Christian Initiation Resources,* edited by Dunning and Reedy, 1:3 (1980): 184–186.

Searles, Wendell. "The RCIA in Your Parish." In *Today's Parish* 12:7 (October 1980): 24–28.

TAPES AND AUDIOVISUALS

Baptism: Initiation into the Christian Community. Sacramental series. New York/Ramsey: Paulist Press, 1976.

Buffalo Office of Worship. *The Conversion Experience.* A filmstrip. Buffalo: Office of Worship, 1982.

Guzie, Tad. *The Radical Rite: The Vision of Christian Initiation of Adults,* cassettes A965, A966, A967. Kansas City, Mo.: NCR Cassettes.

Mitchell, Nathan. *Elements in Catechumenate Formation,* cassette A398. Kansas City, Mo.: NCR Cassettes. Also appears under the title "The Adult Catechumenate in an Age of Pluralism." In *Liturgy* 22:1 (January 1977): 11–17.

Randolph, Therese. *Parish Community: The Ministry of Initiation,* cassette A867. Kansas City, Mo.: NCR Cassettes.

[On Conversion]

Butler, B.D. "Bernard Lonergan and Conversion." In *Worship* 49:6 (June–July 1975): 329–337.

Conn, Walter E. "Conversion: A Developmental Perspective." In *Cross Currents* 3 (Fall 1982): 323–328.

_____ , ed. *Conversion: Perspectives on Personal and Social Transformation.* New York: Alba House, 1978. 330 pp.

Duggan, Robert D. "Conversion: Toward a Better Understanding." In *The Living Light* 18:3 (Fall 1981): 216–224.

Dunning, James B. "Conversion: Reflections on RCIA Revisited." In *Christian Initiation Resources,* edited by Dunning and Reedy, 2:4 (1981).

Fowler, Jim and Sam Keen. *Life Maps: Conversations on the Journey of Faith,* edited by Jerome Berryman. Oak Grove/Minneapolis: Winston Press, 1978. 164 pp.

Griffin, Emilie. *Turning: Reflections on the Experience of Conversion.* New York: Doubleday, 1980. Paperback edition: Image Books, 1982. 219 pp.

Haughton, Rosemary. *The Transformation of Man: A Study of Conversion and Community.* Springfield, Ill.: Templegate, 1967. 280 pp.

Ling, Richard. "The Ecclesial Conversion Process—A Point of View." In *Christian Initiation Resources,* edited by Dunning and Reedy, 2:2 (1981).

Lopresti, James J. "New Christians, New Faith." In *New Catholic World,* vol. 222, no. 1330 (July–August 1979): 164–168.

McBrien, Richard. "Models of Conversion: An Ecclesiological Reflection." In *Living Light* 18:1 (Spring 1981): 7–17.

Searle, Mark. "The Journey of Conversion." In *Worship* 54:1 (January 1980): 35–55.

[On Prayer]

Bernsten, John A. "Christian Affections and the Catechumenate." In *Worship* 52:3 (May 1978): 194–210.

Chilson, Richard. "How to Read and Hear the Word of God." In *Christian Initiation Resources,* edited by Dunning and Reedy, 2:2 (1981).

———. "Initiating Catechumens into the Ways of Christian Prayer." In *The Chicago Catechumenate* 3:5 (July 1981): 6–12.

Lewinski, Ronald. "Speaking of Prayer." In *The Chicago Catechumenate* 2:5 (July 1980): 6–12.

———. "Forming New Catholics in Liturgical Prayer." In *Christian Initiation Resources,* edited by Dunning and Reedy, 3:3 (1983).

[On Celebrations]

Dujarier, Michel. *The Rites of Christian Initiation: Historical and Pastoral Reflections,* translated/edited by Kevin Hart. New York: William H. Sadlier, Inc., 1979. 223 pp.

[On the Rite of Becoming Catechumens]

Driscoll, Richard. "A Book of Catechumens." In *Christian Initiation Resources,* edited by Dunning and Reedy, 2:2 (1981).

Hart, Kevin T. "The Rite of Becoming Catechumens." In *Christian Initiation Resources,* edited by Dunning and Reedy, 1:1 (1980): 34–50.

[On Lent]

O'Hagan, Thomas. "Lent: The Stage of Election and the Period of Enlightenment and Purification." In *Christian Initiation Resources,* edited by Dunning and Reedy, 1:3 (1980): 155–160.

[On the Rite of Election or Enrollment of Names]

Hart, Kevin T. "The Rite of Election." In *Christian Initiation Resources,* edited by Dunning and Reedy, 1:2 (1980): 106–116.

O'Brien, Roger. "Election: A Cathedral Celebration." In *The Chicago Catechumenate* 5:2 (December 1982): 6–10.

Ray, Paul R. and Deece Eckstein. "Rite of Calling: A Celebration of Transition." In *Christian Initiation Resources,* edited by Dunning and Reedy, 3:1 (1982).

[On Exorcisms, Scrutinies, and Presentations]

Fischer, Balthasar. "Baptismal Exorcism in the Catholic Baptismal Rites after Vatican II." In *Studia Liturgica* 10:1 (1974): 48–55.

Lewinski, Ronald. "Scrutiny and Exorcism: The Dynamic of Lent." In *The Chicago Catechumenate* 5:2 (December 1982): 11–15.

Mitchell, Nathan. *The Rites of Exorcism in the Christian Initiation of Adults,* cassette A770. Kansas City, Mo.: NCR Cassettes. Also an edited version, published under the title "Exorcism in the RCIA," appears in *Christian Initiation Resources,* edited by Dunning and Reedy, 1:3 (1980): 161–166.

Parker, James. "Celebrating the Scrutinies." In *Christian Initiation Resources,* edited by Dunning and Reedy, 1:4 (1981): 245–248.

[On the Sacraments of Initiation]

Ciferni, Andrew and Nathan Mitchell. *Christian Initiation,* cassette 870. Kansas City, Mo.: NCR Cassettes.

Gallen, John. "The Pastoral Celebration of Initiation." In *New Catholic World,* vol. 222, no. 1330 (July–August 1979): 148–152.

Lopresti, James J. "Holy Saturday Morning." In *Christian Initiation Resources,* edited by Dunning and Reedy, 1:4 (1981): 241–244. On the preparatory rites.

[On Music for the Rites]

Fragomeni, Richard. "The Music of Baptism: Step by Step." In *Pastoral Music* 6:4 (April–May 1982): 25–27.

Hackett, Joan. "Adult Initiation: Selected Music for Celebrating the Rite." In *Christian Initiation Resources,* edited by Dunning and Reedy, 2:3 (1981).

Periods within the RCIA

[On Inquiry or Precatechumenate]

Barr, Blaine G. and Sandra DeGidio. "How Can a Parish Attract and Interest Inquirers?" In *Christian Initiation*

Resources, edited by Dunning and Reedy, 1:3 (1980): 139–142.

Bauman, William A. "Inquirers in the Parish of the 80s." In *Christian Initiation Resources,* edited by Dunning and Reedy, 1:3 (1980): 143–147.

Bergant, Diane. "The Pre-Catechumenate and the God Who Calls." In *Christian Initiation Resources,* edited by Dunning and Reedy, 2:3 (1981).

Bohr, David. "Evangelization, Conversion, and the RCIA." In *Christian Initiation Resources,* edited by Dunning and Reedy, 1:4 (1981): 259–263.

Boyack, Kenneth. "How to Organize Inquirers?" In *Christian Initiation Resources,* edited by Dunning and Reedy, 1:2 (1980): 86–88.

Dunning, James B. "Christian Initiation: The Period of the Pre-Catechumenate or Inquiry." In *Christian Initiation Resources,* edited by Dunning and Reedy, 1:1 (1980): 20–27.

Hoge, Dean R. "Who Are the Inquirers?" In *Christian Initiation Resources,* edited by Dunning and Reedy, 1:2 (1980): 81–85.

Lewinski, Ronald. "The Pre-Catechumenate: Period of Evangelization." In *Christian Initiation Resources,* edited by Dunning and Reedy, 2:4 (1982).

Weeks, Rene, OP. "Inquiry: The Messy State." In *Christian Initiation Resources,* edited by Dunning and Reedy, 4:1 (1984).

[On the Catechumenate]

Ivory, Thomas P. "The Stages of Initiation: Part II. The Catechumenate." In *Becoming a Catholic Christian,* edited by William J. Reedy, pp. 116–127.

Peterson, Gerald J. "An Initiation Proposed for Deeply Committed Converts." In *Christian Initiation Resources,* edited by Dunning and Reedy, 3:1 (1983).

[On Purification and Enlightenment]

Chilson, Richard W. *A Lenten Pilgrimage—Dying and Rising in the Lord.* New York: Paulist Press, 1983.

Gusmer, Charles W. "Lent—Community Conversion." In *Christian Initiation Resources,* edited by Dunning and Reedy, 1:4 (1981): 235–240.

Parker, James. "The Adult Catechumenate: Pastoral Suggestions for Lent." In *The Living Light* 15:4 (Winter 1978): 476–484.

Ryan, John Barry. "The Baptismal Focus of the Cycle A Lenten Lectionary." In *Christian Initiation Resources,* edited by Dunning and Reedy, 1:2 (1980): 119–122.

[On Mystagogia]

Duggan, Robert D. "Mystagogia and Continuing Conversion." In *Christian Initiation Resources,* edited by Dunning and Reedy, 2:1 (1981).

Dunning, James B. "The Stages of Initiation: Part IV. The Sacraments of Initiation and Afterwards." In *Becoming a Catholic Christian,* edited by William J. Reedy, pp. 135–143.

Gusmer, Charles W. "Celebrating the Easter Season." In *Christian Initiation Resources,* edited by Dunning and Reedy, 3:1 (1982).

Kemp, Raymond B. "Mystagogia—Time to Be Fully Alive." In *Christian Initiation Resources,* edited by Dunning and Reedy, 2:4 (1982).

History

Dix, Gregory, Rev. *The Treatise on the Apostolic Tradition of St. Hippolytus of Rome.* London: S.P.C.K., 1968.

Dujarier, Michel. *A History of the Catechumenate: The First Six Centuries,* translated by Edward J. Hassl. New York: William H. Sadlier, Inc., 1979.

———— . *The Rites of Christian Initiation: Historical and Pastoral Reflections*. New York: William H. Sadlier, Inc., 1979.

Fuller, Reginald. "Christian Initiation in the New Testament." In *Made, Not Born: New Perspectives on Christian Initiation and the Catechumenate,* edited by Robert Hovda, pp. 7–31.

Grant, Robert M. "Development of the Christian Catechumenate." In *Made, Not Born: New Perspectives on Christian Initiation and the Catechumenate,* edited by Robert Hovda, pp. 32–49.

Jungmann, Joseph A. "Catechumenate." In *New Catholic Encyclopedia,* vol. III, pp. 238–240.

Mitchell, Leonel L. "Christian Initiation: The Reformation Period." In *Made, Not Born: New Perspectives on Christian Initiation and the Catechumenate,* edited by Robert Hovda, pp. 83–98.

Mitchell, Nathan D. "Dissolution of the Rite of Christian Initiation." In *Made, Not Born: New Perspectives on Christian Initiation and the Catechumenate,* edited by Robert Hovda, pp. 458–479.

Richardson, Cyril, ed. *Early Christian Fathers,* vol. 1. New York: Macmillan, 1970.

Riley, Hugh. *The Rite of Christian Initiation. A Comparative Study of the Interpretation of the Baptismal Liturgy in the Mystagogical Writings of Cyril of Jerusalem, John Chrysostom, Theodore of Mopsuestia and Ambrose of Milan.* Washington, D.C.: The Catholic University of America Press, 1974, pp. 162–164.

Theology

Ganoczy, Alexander. *Becoming Christian: A Theology of Baptism as the Sacrament of Human History,* translated by John C. Lynch. New York: Paulist Press, 1976. 113 pp.

Guzie, Tad. "Theological Challenges." In *Becoming a Catholic Christian,* edited by William J. Reedy, pp. 165–173.

Hovda, Robert. "Hope for the Future: A Summary." In *Made, Not Born: New Perspectives of Christian Initiation and the Catechumenate,* edited by Hovda, pp. 152–167.

Irwin, Kevin W. "Ecclesiology of Christian Initiation." In *New Catholic World,* vol. 222, no. 1330 (July–August 1979): 176–179.

Ivory, Thomas P. "The Catechumenate: Towards a New Model for the Church." In *Christian Initiation Resources,* edited by Dunning and Reedy, 2:3 (1981).

Kavanagh, Aidan. "Initiation: Baptism and Confirmation." In *Worship* 46:5 (May 1972): 262–278. Reprinted in *The Sacraments: Readings in Contemporary Sacramental Theology,* edited by Michael J. Taylor. Staten Island: Alba House, 1981, pp. 81–94.

Keifer, Ralph. "Christian Initiation: State of the Question." In *Worship* 48:7 (August–September 1974): 392–404. Reprinted in *Made, Not Born: New Perspectives on Christian Initiation and the Catechumenate,* edited by Robert Hovda, pp. 138–151.

———. "Faith Community Necessary for Adult Initiation." In *New Catholic World,* vol. 222, no. 1330 (July–August 1979): 161–163.

LaVerdiere, Eugene A. "The Rite of Christian Initiation of Adults: A New Testament Introduction." In *Christian Initiation Resources,* edited by Dunning and Reedy, 3:1 (1982).

Worgul, George. "The Ecclesiology of 'the Rite of Christian Initiation of Adults.' " In *Louvain Studies* 6:2 (Fall 1976): 159–169.

Implementation

Baltimore Division of Liturgy. *Packet on the RCIA.* Baltimore: Division of Liturgy, 1979.

Boyack, Kenneth. *A Parish Guide to Adult Initiation*. Ramsey, N.J.: Paulist Press, 1979. 106 pp.

Cincinnati Archdiocese. *Christian Initiation of Adults: Materials Packet*. Cincinnati: Religious Education Office and Worship Office, 1978.

Curtin, Rosalie and others. *RCIA: A Practical Approach to Christian Initiation for Adults*. Dubuque: Wm. C. Brown Publishers, 1981. 131 pp.

Dubuque Archdiocese. *RCIA: Foundations of Christian Initiation*. (Commissioned by the Archdiocese of Dubuque.) Dubuque: Wm. C. Brown Publishers, 1982. 89 pp.

Lewinski, Ronald. *Welcoming the New Catholic*. Chicago: Liturgy Training Publications, 1978 (1980). 47 pp.

Ling, Richard, ed. *A Resource Collection of Initiation Aids*. Lakewood, Colo.: Worship Resources.

Truitt, Gordon E. *The Shape of the Journey: A Parish Guide to Initiation*. A 12-part serialization beginning with vol. 12:1 (January 1983) of *Celebration: A Creative Worship Service*. Kansas City, Mo.: National Catholic Reporter Publishing Company.

[On Sponsors]

Dowd, Mary. "Witness and Guide: The Role of Sponsors in RCIA." In *Christian Initiation Resources,* edited by Dunning and Reedy, 1:3 (1980): 146–154.

Kansas City/St. Joseph Office of Worship. *Adult Initiation—Sponsor's Role*. Kansas City, Mo.: Office of Worship, 1977. 7 pp.

Lewinski, Ronald. *Guide for Sponsors*. Chicago: Liturgy Training Publications, 1980. 54 pp.

Ling, Richard. *Sponsors RCIA*. Lakewood, Colo.: Worship Resources, 1978. 10 pp.

[On Ministries]

Komadina, Sharon. "Vision and Leadership in the RCIA." In *Christian Initiation Resources,* edited by Dunning and Reedy, 2:2 (1981).

Randolph, Therese. "Companions for the Journey: The Ministering Community in the RCIA." In *New Catholic World,* vol. 22, no. 1330 (July–August 1979): 153–156.

Vertreace, Martha M. "Lay Ministries for the RCIA." In *The Chicago Catechumenate* 4:3 (February 1982): 5–10.

Villaca, Theophille and Michel Dujarier. "The Various Ministries in Christian Initiation." In *Becoming a Catholic Christian,* edited by William J. Reedy, pp. 144–155.

Catechumenate for Children/Youth

Lewinski, Ronald. "A Catechumenate for Youth." In *Christian Initiation Resources,* edited by Dunning and Reedy, 1:4 (1981): 219–223.

——— . "Towards a Children's Catechumenate." In *Christian Initiation Resources,* edited by Dunning and Reedy, 3:1 (1982).

Villaca, Theophille and Michel Dujarier. "Working Principles for a Children's Catechumenate." In *The Chicago Catechumenate* 4:5 (July 1982): 19–22.